WINNER OF THE DEBORAH SAMPSON PRIZE FOR WOMEN'S MILITARY WRITING

# DARKER
## THAN
## NAVY BLUE

### A SAILOR'S
### MEMOIR OF
### TRAGEDY AND
### HEALING

THANK You
For ReADiNG !!!
Nic
USN, 29 OCT 18

### NICOLE
### STRONG

ISBN: 978-1-943258-95-6 (soft)
         978-0-9960506-4-7 (hard)

Strong. Nicole.
Darker than Navy Blue

Edited by: Tracy Crow

Charlotte, NC
www.warrenpublishing.net
Printed in the United States

*For Neil—*
*Fair winds and following seas, Shipmate.*
*You are eternally missed.*

# PRAISE FOR
## *DARKER THAN NAVY BLUE*

"*Strong's intimate and unflinching search for deeper personal truths leads toward a deeper inner awareness about the role of childhood trauma on young adulthood decision-making, and why victims of childhood abuse find it more difficult to report abuse by those who hold positions of military power.* In Darker than Navy Blue, *Strong personifies the mettle of strength and fortitude perhaps necessary to break free, finally, of the victim cycle before the cycle irreparably breaks the spirit.*"

—TRACY CROW,
FORMER US MARINE CORPS OFFICER AND
AUTHOR/EDITOR OF FIVE MILITARY-THEMED BOOKS

"*Nicole Strong is every parent's daughter, betrayed and abused by her military guardians in power, she survived of her own will, with some help from a friend. It took years to heal the damage, from early childhood and the US Navy. Hers is a Cassandra voice come to life in the 21st Century.*"

—GEORGE R. BROADHEAD,
US MARINE CORPS/RETIRED. AUTHOR OF
ONGOING SERIES OF ARTICLES ON VETERANS IN
BROOKLYN, NEW YORK COMMUNITY, AMERICAN ARTIST
MAGAZINE; POETRY IN NEWSPAPERS AND MAGAZINES.
AWARDED THE SILVER STAR AND PURPLE HEART MEDALS.

"*A haunting story of sexual trauma in the military,* Strong's Darker Than Navy Blue *sets a tone of self-contempt without self-pity. Tightly winding together her military career and subsequent struggle with self, Strong provides a rare look at women in the military that is simultaneously heartbreaking and hopeful in its depiction of what women endure in the name of duty, honor, and country.*"

—BROOKE KING,
IRAQ-WAR VETERAN AND AUTHOR OF
A FORTHCOMING MEMOIR FROM POTOMAC BOOKS

# AUTHOR'S NOTE

This true story required a significant level of collaboration, and would not have been possible without the generous support of my husband and fellow shipmates.

Because of the trauma I faced during my military service and afterward during recovery, I did not want to only draw from personal memory. To produce a memoir as close to the truth as possible, I relied on transcripts and consulted with shipmates. What you are about to read is the most accurate recreation of events possible, to include the recreation of conversations. I am so grateful that I had so many facets to draw upon in the writing of this harrowing ordeal.

However, all names have been changed to protect everyone's privacy, including the namesake and legacy of our ship.

# PROLOGUE

# Memories in the Box

On this particular day, I am holding a small brown box that, from the outside, looks just as it is: a pintsized-corrugated cardboard container that's worn from years of use, multiple moves, and long-term storage. But inside are the precious few items remaining from my short years of US Navy service. This box has become my haphazard seachest of sorts, and today I'm carrying the tiny collection from the basement to my bedroom. For too long, I have been unable to glance over at the box without sensing the level of anxiety that causes one's hair to rise on her arms. *Today will be different*, I tell myself on the way to my bedroom. *Today I am ready to face all this.* But when I open the box, I am flooded with memories over a decade old. I have to remind myself, yet again, that I am no longer that young woman—that I am safe and that I am a completely different person today.

The first thing I see is the dented silver belt buckle with an Arleigh Burke destroyer and the engraving, *plankowner*, under it. Beneath all this is a small stack of photographs. In one, I'm wearing the *smurf*—the ubiquitous blue boot camp sweater with gold *Navy* written across it, and on my head is a friend's white dress cover, called a *dixie cup*, that I was wearing as a joke.

Another photograph reveals the younger version of me in red coveralls, standing with fellow sailors outside the fire school at Whidbey Island, Washington. My short, curvy figure stands out against their tall masculine ones, yet I managed to fit in. We were a cohesive and hardworking team for the short time I was there, teaching aircraft firefighting to classes of various ships and squadrons.

In another photograph, I'm dressed in heavily insulated firefighting gear and holding a large torch for lighting the black metal airplane frame for a firefighting training exercise. Other pictures capture memories of my ship and the Panama Canal.

Then I see my stack of folded discharge papers, the notorious DD-214s that tell only part of the story that has become the caliginous mangled remains of three years of my life. At first, I roughly cast them aside. I didn't want to look at them, or the additional comments supplied by the commanding officer of my first and only ship. Eventually, I unfold them, because even this is still a part of the *story* of me, even if it's an ugly story, and in the past.

My eyes scan over the cold black words, and for the first time in a decade, I don't feel the hurt as I used to. I don't take so personal anymore the biting adjectives my CO used to justify an *other than honorable* discharge. These ugly words no longer define me. Besides, underneath this discharge is the truer version—the honorable upgrade that took me half a decade of fighting Navy bureaucracy to achieve. The truth is that I dealt with way more than most of my fellow shipmates ever knew, and I carried the terrible weight of this truth for as long as I could. When I finally did collapse underneath the pressure and revealed the ugly truth about sexual assaults aboard our ship, I was the one pinned as the guilty party by men who outranked me and who didn't want fingers pointed in their direction.

All the darkness aside, I did get to see and do some really neat things in the Navy, though not nearly as much as I'd wanted to. I wanted to go on deployments, and become a *shellback* crossing the Equator. I wanted to party in Australia and Hong Kong, and see the beautiful sites of different cultures foreign to the one I grew up in. For years the disappointment weighed heavy, but even that weight has been lifted, thanks to years of hard work that included therapy and lots of self-examination.

In the end, I realize what really matters most are the many shipmates I served with. My shipmates and our memories together now form the stable thoughts I try to hold on to these days.

I am not the first woman in the Navy, let alone in the military, who has had to work hard over the years to deal with the shackles of heavy emotions, especially the guilt and shame that are attached to military sexual trauma. Today, I understand that the turn my career took was in many ways beyond my control, and I have resigned myself not to continue to compartmentalize and numb everything inside me, even as this box of memories sits neatly in my hands. The weight in my hands is real, as real as the memories inside me. No longer can I shelve the pain and loss. I have learned to face these things, and so I flip through the random collection of everything that is in this box.

I look over my dog tags, my first ship's ballcap—and that's when I see *them*: my set of military dress medals.

The first medal is the orange, blue, and yellow national defense medal given to everyone who serves. Most sailors call this one the *boot camp* medal since most of us receive it to wear at boot camp graduation. Next to this medal is the one that truly means something to me—a dark blue and green rifle expert medal that I earned on Whidbey Island.

The medals sit atop a photograph of me in my full dress blues taken by a photographer friend of mine. At first all I see is the proud look of a woman sailor. On second glance, the look on my face is all at once full of pain, resilience, strength, and massive, crushing loss.

When I lift the medals from the box, they clink against one another, and I am taken back in time to that fateful day fifteen years earlier when I was ordered to appear before my ship's commanding officer at Captain's Mast, which is one of the more revolting of the old traditions still practiced by the Navy. There I'd marched in my dress uniform with my medals chiming against each other, and stood at the position of attention in front of shipmates while our CO berated me for many things that were not my fault and were beyond my control. Not once did he mention that I had endured an entire year of being stalked, harassed, and sexually assaulted by senior ranking men in my chain of command. Instead, I stood there, listening to his list of lies that, at the time, seemed to mirror the lies that each senior-ranking sailor had used to keep me from telling the truth about their behavior. The lie? That I had no credibility, and that no one would believe me. After a while, I'd told myself the biggest lie of all: that if I just pretended none of this was happening to me, maybe it wasn't happening at all.

With clarity given to me after years of extensive therapy and nonstop self-help reading, I realize now that the hardest lie to overcome was the one that no one would believe me. This was the lie that had formed early in my childhood by an abusive uncle, and reinforced years later in the Navy when I did finally report the strings of sexual assaults, only to be blamed for them. Far easier, as it turned out to be for our CO, to blame a young woman sailor for the corruption within his command than to deal with a handful of corrupt leaders who had served the Navy far longer than she, and who were counting on a Navy retirement. After all, how would it look to the CO's commanding officer if it could be proven that the ship's senior enlisted sailors were abusing their power, even grooming their victims for sexual assaults?

For years I was so close to being a ghost of myself, floating almost transparently through life in a haze, wanting often to just end my life by my own hand because I couldn't stop reliving everything, and couldn't stop feeling angry. Rage was the only way I knew how to handle anything, so I felt that I was a burden to my family. Wouldn't suicide serve as a kinder option for us all?

Of course, I realize now how wrong that thinking was. Eventually I learned how to rethink my past and my abusers. Every time I allow myself to rise above the trees, so to speak, to look down upon the forest, I grant myself a fuller picture of my Navy experience—an experience that also includes happy memories and the support of many shipmates who have stepped forth since that Captain's Mast, and with versions of the truth that align with mine. I am no longer as alone as I felt for so long, and I am grateful.

But I will never forget that fateful day of Captain's Mast, standing in the rain to wait for a door to open and for my name to be called. I will always vividly remember how miserable and lonely I was that day, more than I had ever been in my life or ever wish to be again. I have compassion for the jaded young woman I was after the vicious Captain's Mast. After all, I was exhausted from being chased by a handful of forty-something-year-old men and the weight of their threats and lies.

# CHAPTER 1

# The Phone Call: Captain's Mast

It's October 16, 2002, and I'm relaxing in my barracks room on Whidbey Island in northwestern Washington State after a long, busy day teaching aircraft fire fighting. On the nightstand next to me a small, black flip phone begins ringing, breaking the tranquility of the moment. I quickly answer the phone. "Strong," the woman says, her gravelly voice filled with irritation or contempt. I'm not sure which yet, but inside the brief pause I recognize the voice as the one belonging to my ship's master-at-arms. I stand up, sensing the urgency of her unexpected call. "You are going to have to pack all your stuff and get back down here to Everett tomorrow. You are going to Captain's Mast tomorrow morning. Be here at 8 a.m. sharp."

"What? Why?" I choke out.

"Listen, I don't ask questions. I just have to tell you that you are ordered to pack all your things and be at the shipyard next to Naval Station Everett at zero-eight-hundred in full dress blues. Don't be late. Trust me, you don't need me to tell you what happens if you're late." Her warning resonates deep inside me. I get the point.

I hang up the phone and sit down on the bed. I'm stunned. Numb. Feeling a tad sucker-punched. Heaven only knows what *this* troubling call means. The very words themselves, *Captain's Mast*, are enough to induce panic within any sailor. Captain's Mast means I'm going to have to stand before the commanding officer of my ship and give an account of whatever offenses he feels I've committed. He doesn't need any evidence, and I don't get a chance to defend myself. Basically suspicion, alone, is enough to convict at Captain's Mast.

After a long sleepless night and a one-hour drive south, I'm standing outside a building, straight as a board at the position of attention, waiting for my name to be called. Inside, most of my fellow shipmates are gathered in rows of chairs, with the commanding officer of our ship seated at the front. I have no idea what military charges have been officially brought against me, or what my fellow shipmates have been coerced into believing and reporting. But I am soon to find out.

At some point, the mental weight of this moment forces me to close my eyes. For how long, I can't say. But when rain falls like soft taps on the shoulders of my dark gabardine dress uniform, I finally open my eyes again and allow another look at Puget Sound. Across the sound, I can make out the foggy shape of Whidbey Island in the distance that has been home to me for the past couple of months. As I marvel at how beautiful everything is the realization hits me with a wave of dread that I'm finally here, standing alone, waiting anxiously in a muddy shipyard in Everett, Washington. Waiting for one single door to my whole life to open.

Who could have imagined that a young woman could be blamed for the rape and sexual harassment that had been happening to her at the hands of senior enlisted men? But this is exactly what I'm about to discover. In this moment, however, I'm standing in shock, at what looks like America yet feels like an alien world in which my worst nightmares are about to become realized. For the past year I had put up with pretty abhorrent things. A handful of men ranked high above me had said and done some awful things to me, and after fighting to resist this treatment and seeing what these men did in retribution, I soon realized reporting anything was futile.

What also proved futile was the thinking that I could simply lock all these ugly secrets and lies inside and pretend everything was normal, and therein was my deepest moral dilemma. Looking back I had no choice either way. The soft voice of reason echoing behind everything in the back of my mind was my best friend Dave's warning. He had foreseen all this a long time ago, telling me that when this whole mess came crashing down that I would be the one burned under the collapsed remains.

But to keep going every day I convinced myself that something good would come of this. After all, if we actually believe the end will be terribly painful how far are any of us willing to walk the various aspects of our life journeys?

I recall the first Captain's Mast onboard this ship, and the chaos, finger pointing, and ass chewing that unfolds and frames everything. I know the fact that I am standing outside this door to just such an event means that this is far from okay. But I will not run. I am no coward. I stand proudly, with military bearing, even amidst the storm raging inside my heart, watching the sunrise above the clouds and fog over the sound. I stare out at the misty wall of evergreens standing on Whidbey Island, my mind pleading with silent screams, wishing I had wings to fly away up into the stars I know are over the ocean.

I am twenty-three. I should feel young, yet deep inside I feel as roughly aged as discarded barn wood left outside in the elements. Above me the heavy gray sky is spitting teeny miserable raindrops everywhere. I shiver as I realize my warm service dress blues clash with the fellow sailors in working dungarees and windbreakers walking by.

My fellow shipmates seem to know what is about to take place as they turn their heads to catch glimpses. Some of them point and shake their heads in disgust. Their disgust hits me like a spike. I am beginning to suspect that the nightmare that kept me from reporting rampant abuses of power might have come true: that I will become the scapegoat for this entire horrible situation.

It's still raining, even harder, and I dare to break attention long enough to look up. The large cold drops hit hard against my face. The sky may be crying, but I swear that I'll not allow a single tear to fall in front of them. I refuse to show any weakness. I am holding onto hope, no matter how false, that everything might turn out in my favor.

Next to me is a set of stairs going up into the building, and on the other side stands a small group of men. They are also wearing their Dress Blues, the eponymous "cracker jacks," and stand at attention. Some are good friends; one is my best friend. Another is here because he deserves to be. Why we all are here is a very long terrible story, but here we are waiting for the short and abrupt ending of Captain's Mast.

When the single door loudly swings open, my heart skips a beat. The ship's master-at-arms steps out smartly and shouts, "DCFN Strong! Front and center, now!"

And so it begins.

Only one person—my best friend, Dave—had rightly predicted an outcome that would include a public shaming. Somehow Dave had known how the chips would fall, and he'd warned me. And now, as I walk up the stairs I pass him. His large shape stands stoically at attention, his face flushed deep crimson with what I recognize as anger, contrasted with the bright white *dixie cup* or sailor's hat nestled two fingers high on his brow.

I move as I have been instructed, walking swiftly around and past the men standing in their crackerjack dress uniforms with black neckerchiefs flapping in the soft wind and dress medals that quietly clink. I start slowly up the single flights of wooden stairs and as I step inside I notice two large rows of dozens of shipmates seated on either side of me. So it's true: everyone not on duty has been ordered to attend this Captain's Mast.

The chiming of my two medals is a soft golden bell announcing every step I take as I walk forward. I walk up the long aisle between the rows of staring shipmates to a raised platform with a podium. Behind the podium stands the CO, and his hateful glare is undeniable. When I hear the command to halt, I'm standing at attention in front of his scowl.

# CHAPTER 2

## Several Years Earlier

How I ended up in the Navy was an adventure itself.
I graduated from high school in 1998 with no real idea what I wanted to do, so I bounced around the country. For several months I lived and worked in a monastery outside Pittsburgh. Afterward, I moved on to missionary work in Mobile, Alabama. After surviving fire ants and a small hurricane, I realized I wanted to return north to Missouri to be near family, so I settled on a job as a Union painter's apprentice.

Construction is predominantly a man's field, and the way to earn respect is through hustle. During that one year as a painter's apprentice I learned how to run sharp fast cut-ins with large Purdy brushes, paint six-panel doors flawlessly with gloss paint, and roll endless walls. What I learned most, however, was the importance of keeping up with the men, despite my obvious lack of experience and five-foot-tall stature.

But when the economy unexpectedly dropped in 2000, the entire country plunged into a recession—not that I knew what a recession was back then. I just knew I was laid off and pregnant with my first child. The brief relationship with her father had ended violently, but looking back I am glad it ended, period. I had no idea how deep he had been into drugs and alcohol, and it would have been a terrible place for me, let alone our daughter. But when the unemployment checks ran out soon after she was born, and with no job prospects or money, I decided it was best for my daughter to provide her with a more stable home through adoption. I'll never forget the last time I held her in my arms, and I can still feel her newborn skin under the kiss I gave her just before handing her to her new mom and dad. The only peace or comfort in the moment was sensing that I was acting from a selfless place of responsibility for my daughter's sake. Maybe I couldn't fix my jobless situation, but I could ensure that my daughter was safe, and living in a stable situation.

Not long after my daughter's adoption, a good friend asked if I'd considered joining the military. I hadn't. "Well, you should," she said, looking at me with warm, caring eyes. This was June 2000, and as I looked outside the window of her house I could see the green grass, daffodils, and tree buds popping up everywhere. I realized I needed to do something with my life. I was carrying around a broken heart for a number of reasons that I hadn't allowed myself time to reflect upon, but the time would come eventually to face it all. Outside spring was on the way, and so, apparently, was my own rebirth of sorts. My friend must have sensed this too. She was much older, and with gentle insistence that day added, "You have to do something, right?" The soothing sound of her voice spoke a logic that I understood. I had provided my daughter with a best-life option, but I hadn't yet dared to imagine what a best-life option would look like for me.

For some time afterward, I couldn't stop thinking about the idea of a military career. My father always had a deep respect for the military, especially the Navy; he took me onboard USS Missouri as a young child when we lived in Everett, Washington. Between the ages of two and five I was going to bases for air shows, or going along to the local airport with my dad and uncle outside Everett where we would watch the National Guard run flight drills. Years later, I could still hear the loud, distinct thump of Chinook helicopters doing training exercises at Paine Field; so unforgettable, that I would know with no doubt what that sound was no matter where I was so many years later in the Navy.

Military service ran in my family: grandfathers, uncles, even my mother. Since my mother's service had been marred by hardships and trials I wasn't surprised to find she wasn't keen on the idea of my enlisting. My father, however, was excited about the idea. My mom decided to play it neutral; she didn't encourage or dissuade. She knew her rebellious daughter would learn more from a snake bite than a warning about snakes. So, before too long there I was, walking into a recruiter's office, ready to enlist.

The Marines had always intrigued me. Maybe it was their reputation for hardness. And maybe it was the fact that there were no Marines in my family, but it didn't hurt that theirs was the first office I saw when I walked in. I took a deep breath as I opened door number one. The recruiter's head, bent over paperwork on his desk, looked up in surprise as I walked in. "What can I do for you?" He stood, and I got an eyeful of his smartly tailored dress blues, the dark, high-necked jacket and blue pants with that storied "blood" stripe. He looked impressive, so sure of himself and his purpose, and I was struck speechless for a moment. When I found my voice, "I am interested in enlisting." I tried to appear more confident than I really felt.

"Well," he said, thrusting his chest forward enough so that all the medals smacked heavily against each other in a discordant crashing manner, "I am not interested in females joining my Corps."

I had assumed recruiters were hungry for willing people like me. I felt my cheeks growing hot with anger. "Listen," I said, trying to reason with him, "I want to do this. I'm twenty years old, and I'm in great physical shape. I know I'm a woman, but I more than pull my own weight."

He shook his head, grabbed some papers, and walked to the door, shutting off the light, as a way to make obvious his point. Outside his office, he locked the door and said, "No offense. I can't do anything for you." He pointed to a back wall with another door. "The Air Force can help you out. Good luck." And with that he smartly turned and walked away, his handsome dress uniform now becoming the color of my smashed words and thoughts, the red stripe of his pants the color of the blood draining from my shocked face, the fading chime of his medals sounding like the note of finality.

The Marine recruiter might have closed one door, but I was dauntless.

I had grown up pushing open doors or finding a way around closed-door obstacles with noted resilience. The first time I was two years old, and the obstacle was a set of stairs. My mom had taken me to my grandmother's house for a visit. They had set me down for a nap and were having coffee when something went flying by their peripheral vision. Gram-mama looked at my mom and said, "Did you see that?" a second before the blood-curdling scream. They ran to find that I had taken my toddler bike and flown down the flight of stairs. Actually, I had flown over the stairs, having worked up a considerable amount of speed that enabled me to maintain an outstanding arc and trajectory. I'd miss the stairs altogether, sailing over them and landing at the feet of a pale, surprised uncle.

I don't recall this but Gram-mama swears up and down it happened, and that this is where I earned my name "Niki-Knievel" after the daredevil himself. She added that fresh after landing, there I was, trying to drag the bike back up the stairs, wanting to do it again. She always maintained that tenacity and fearlessness were running gears in the cogs that made me tick. Looking back, I concede she might have been the first one in my life to really know who I was at my core.

And indeed, that plucky determination only became more outstanding and fiery as I got older. I had no fear with obstacles. And this door closing by a Marine recruiter was like any other closed door. I just had to make minor adjustments. So I pushed open the door leading me into the office with the Air Force.

The Air Force recruiters were a mismatched pair; one was a terribly overweight guy in a blue uniform so tight fitting he fidgeted uncomfortably in his chair. The other recruiter was tall and thin. His uniform, equally ill-fitted, hung too loose. The tall, thin recruiter was the one who did most of the talking, speaking fast with bird-like movements. As he spoke of how much he loved being stationed in one place for his first four-year enlistment, I reflected upon my mom's time in the Air Force, and how she'd felt stuck in one unhappy place at a stuffy federal building in the middle of a large city. I didn't want that. I wanted to see the world.

Besides, standing next to these guys, I became aware of how much I hated their uniforms. I was recalling the way they smelled when burned, remembering the day my mom took her bulging garment bag, ripped it open on the front lawn, and fed every single piece of clothing it contained into a large bonfire after she got her discharge papers. So maybe in a rare moment of solidarity with my mother, I decided the Air Force wasn't for me.

Still I let them administer the ASVAB entry test. After answering what seemed like pages and pages of crazy engineering diagrams, endless off-the-wall questions, and row-upon-row of random codes and mathematical equations I left the testing room feeling as if I had failed.

Turns out I had scored high, so high that the Air Force recruiters were almost knocking each other over trying to excitedly talk me into signing papers that minute. But they were too pushy, and I'd decided for once to side with my mother when it came to the Air Force, so I left, politely excusing myself and walking out of the office just as a Navy recruiter ran into me knocking me down.

"Oh, pardon me," he said. "Are you okay?" He sounded peppy and happy, and was wearing those handsome working whites I recalled strikingly from Top Gun. I forgave him immediately as he helped me up.

"I'm okay."

"Do you need anything?"

"Well, actually, I'm looking to enlist."

"Really? I'd be happy to help you with that." He seemed like a nice guy. He was about five inches taller than me, trim, with short blond hair, dark blue eyes, and a good demeanor. There was something genuine and trustworthy about him, and this reached out and grabbed me. He was the kind of guy I would happily buy a used car from.

I shared my ASVAB scores as we both took a seat at his desk. "Oh wow," he said. "You scored extremely well. You could do anything—work in any rating with the exception of nuclear machinist mate."

"Huh?" I was confused.

"Well, rating is another word for job in the Navy," he explained. I was also told that I could do just about any job, with the exception of the SEALs, and the nuclear science field. But women like me, he said, could be Navy divers and explosive ordinance disposal technicians, and my future was suddenly sounding brighter than I'd ever dared to imagine possible.

I looked up at the recruiting posters on the wall with LET THE JOURNEY BEGIN written in huge block letters above the image of a cutting edge warship. This was like something out of the Tom Clancy novels I began reading when I was seven.

My mind was made up. *This fits*, I thought.

In the back of my mind I could even hear Kenny Loggin's "Danger Zone" begin to play, and I found myself saying, "Okay, I want to sign up. What do I do next?" The experience, in a way, was part surreal. Was I really enlisting in the Navy?

Yes. And I really wanted to.

The Navy recruiter went to work on my enlistment package. Over the next few weeks and after several discussions I chose damage controlman, or naval firefighter, over a job with gas turbine engines. As the recruiter explained, this was just a source rating for what I really wanted to do, which was to go to Navy dive school and end up as an EOD technician, dismantling bombs or mines.

My dad, a former volunteer firefighter, was excited about my job choice. He was bubbling over with mirth, but my mother was quiet. A certain heaviness had settled upon her as she stood in the background of our conversations. She never once said, "Don't do this," but I know now that she had hated the idea of my enlisting because she knew better than my father what was waiting for me on the other side, though not even she could have seen that in three short years my military career would end in the biggest ball of flames any of us had ever seen.

But in August 2000, I found it equally exciting and frightening to be standing in a room with other enlistees and committing five years of my life to the Navy, and uttering an oath to defend the Constitution against all enemies foreign and domestic. A month later, I left for boot camp.

Look, I knew the Navy wasn't going to be easy, but I had been working in a man's world in construction the past year, and the hundreds of men I worked around had always been pretty respectful. They looked at me as an equal. So, I thought I was ready to join the man's world that is the Navy. How different or hard could it be?

# CHAPTER 3

# US Navy Boot Camp

I was twenty-one when I reported for eight weeks of boot camp in Great Lakes, Illinois, September 2000. Great Lakes Training Center, or "Great Mistakes" as the base is better known in the Navy, has trained new recruits outside Chicago for over a hundred years, and in the 1990s had become the only boot camp location for the Navy. Many sailors consider it the place they first realize the horrible mistake of enlisting. I would never have that regret, in spite of the trials I would go through.

I never questioned why the words "boot camp" are used to describe basic training. And, after having gone through boot camp, I think it sounds much nicer than "kick-your-ass-camp," which is actually a better description.

Navy boot camp might not be as physically demanding as what the Marines or Army go through, but to any civilian thrown into this mix, boot camp is boot camp, and there's no quitting once your name is on the dotted line and your backside is in the hands of the Recruit Division Commanders or RDCs—the Navy version of drill instructors.

The RDCs yelled at us, picked on us individually, and then marched us and made us drop for countless push-ups and eight-count body-builders for small infractions. We were expected to learn and use only proper nautical language, along with the old Navy colloquialisms thrown in. The words *attention to detail*, *reveille*, and *military bearing*, along with the other favorite non-stop sayings of the RDCs to *Hurry the fuck up and quit dickin' the dog* would become well defined for every one of us, with the sounds of David Grey's album *White Ladder* playing endlessly on one of their radios. Apparently, the RDCs had hobbies other than cursing and screaming all the time, and at least one of them had great taste in music. Some of these somber themes perfectly fit the overall miserable condition of the place.

In the middle of boot camp a disaster occurred that I will never forget. On October 12, the RDCs stopped training to tell us the grave news: USS Cole (DDG-67) had just been bombed by al-Qaeda terrorists in the waters outside the Middle Eastern country, Yemen. USS Cole was being refueled as a small watercraft approached off of her port side and suddenly exploded killing seventeen sailors and injuring thirty-nine in the attack.

This shook every single one of us as we sat with our RDCs in ten minutes of silence. We had never known anything but safety in our young lives, so the idea of a fatal attack on one of our more cutting-edge ships was a wake-up call for all of us, including the RDC's.

After this their attitude drastically changed; if we were about to enter a war against terrorism, we needed to be ready for what we would face. For all its challenges, boot camp suddenly became even tougher. And no one complained. We knew why and we knew what was at stake.

Under their stern leadership, we changed from sheltered spoiled kids into proper sailors. We had to learn how to take orders, and to become doers not thinkers. Even in our sleep as they say, we had to become an organized cohesive group that could fight fires and get a ship fired up and out to sea.

The RDCs made sure we were thoroughly indoctrinated on the chain of command, and our place in relation to it. We learned about all the ranks and rates, starting with E1 through E3. One huge myth is that anyone in the Navy is a "seaman," which actually could not be further from the truth. All seamen are sailors, but not all sailors are seamen. One is actually a fireman, seaman, constructionman, airman, or a hospitalman depending on what area his rating or job originates. As a damage controlman, my area would be in engineering; therefore, I was now a "fireman." As an E-1 my new title was DCFR—damage controlman fireman recruit.

But the official step into a leadership position happens when a person makes it into the petty officer ranks E-4 to E-6. When a sailor makes petty officer, he or she starts out as a 3rd class, wearing a "crow" or rate badge on their left arms consisting of one single red chevron beneath a white embroidered eagle. Then when they make 2nd class they put on a new crow with two chevrons. 1st classes wear a crow with three chevrons—symbolic of the most authority among the junior enlisted.

Under the "crow" on one's left sleeve is the symbol reflecting one's job in the Navy; as a damage controlman my symbol was a crossed fire axe and maul.

One outstanding thing I must note about the Navy is pride in one's job rate and one's rank: sailors take their title and rank seriously. From boatswain's mates, or BMs, who keep the exterior of the ship neat, or the gunner's mates, or GMs, who are responsible for loading the five-inch gun on the front of the ship, to the engine men, or ENs, who run and maintain diesel engines and other auxiliary equipment, there are over fifty different job ratings. Every job has its vital role in the Navy. Above junior enlisted petty officers are the senior enlisted ranks E-7 though E-9, who are known as the chiefs, senior chiefs, and master chiefs. The Navy is unique from other service branches in that senior enlisted pay grades E-7 through E-9 are authorized to wear the same khaki uniform as navy officers.

I was surprised to find out that Navy officers are not the ones who hold all the power. It's chiefs and above who really run everything. Ultimately, a chief's primary role is not just to take care of his or her people, but also to train the officers from ranks O-1 to O-4. When a commanding officer asks a question or needs to gain advice regarding a leadership issue, it is highly likely that a chief will provide the answers. So, chiefs have a huge responsibility in the Navy, and with this comes an almost god-like respect that places them above officers in almost all cases.

But the fact remains they are still enlisted, yet look almost like an officer at first sight since they wear the same khaki uniform. The mistake of saluting chiefs is actually an easily made one but an insult for which they have no sense of humor whatsoever.

I found this out the hard way near the end of boot camp. I was going to medical and made the sorry mistake of saluting someone walking past me in khakis before seeing the anchors that differentiated her from an officer. I'll never forget that feeling in the pit of my stomach as I realized my mistake at the same time she did. She stopped, turned, and shouted, "Recruit! About face, Recruit!"

I stopped dead in my tracks, knowing I had been caught, and turned around to face the chief. I snapped to attention as she began to unravel on me.

"Recruit! Did you just salute me?"

"Yes, Chief! I did!" I was beginning to shake, knowing there was a high probability this was not going to end well.

"What the hell is wrong with your damn eyes, Recruit? Don't you see these anchors?" She pushed up the anchors on her lapel closer to my face so I could see them better.

"Yes, Chief! I do now!"

"Good! That means I work for a damn living, Recruit! Now drop! Push the ground until I get tired!"

So I dropped, and did about fifty decent pushups before she called me to stand up.

Getting back on my feet I pulled myself together to stand at attention.

"Do you know what the difference between a chief and an officer is now?"

"Yes, Chief! I do."

"Good. Now, carry on!"

And with that I had my first real run in with a chief. I had no idea it would not be my last. In fact it was a foreshadowing of the running issues I would have with chiefs, and how much they would frighten me with their power and authority.

Two long months of boot camp went by the fastest and slowest I have ever seen time pass, until we were finally at the end, wearing dress blues and marching with thousands of other brand new sailors at our huge graduation in December.

After graduation, I moved across the street from boot camp to Service School Command (SSC) for training as a firefighter.

# CHAPTER 4

# Becoming a Firefighter

Damage Control "A" school was located on the far end of the base, in a nice new building overlooking Lake Michigan.

My class was assigned two instructors to whom we answered as our direct chain-of-command. When they came into our classroom to introduce themselves it was like meeting Laurel and Hardy; our first instructor was a DC1 or 1st class damage controlman with three bright gold chevrons sticking out on his arm. He was a tall and thin guy, stern, with bushy short hair and a large mustache.

Then we met our other instructor, a DCC, or damage control chief; a short, extremely stocky guy with a large bald head and strong jaw. The curious thing about Chief was that his dress blues had five red service stripes on his left forearm, one stripe for every four years, under his crow. Every one of us whispered about this, and then we all understood what this meant: at some point the chief had gotten in trouble. A chief with twenty years in the Navy normally had five gold service stripes on his forearm and three gold chevrons on the crow on his upper left arm sleeve, which sailors joke around to mean they haven't been caught yet; the gold denoting continuous years of good conduct, which a person gets after twelve years of service. But if they've been caught doing something they shouldn't have, those gold stripes go back to red in a flash. Most chiefs with that much time in who bear red stripes are quietly respected because it means they're unwilling to put up with crap, or kiss-ass to make their way through the world at large. Eventually, near the end of school I would get curious enough and bold enough to ask Chief about his red stripes, but I was too busy learning in the meantime to bother.

In class there was a lot of information and endless memorization of basic shipboard firefighting, which was a challenge I rather enjoyed. I was that person who gulped everything down and asked endless questions, and this irritated some of the guys because it made me look too motivated, and made them feel complacent. Maybe they weren't really so complacent but I definitely was motivated. I was excited to be there, and I wanted to exceed the standards set before me.

It was a shock realizing that the standards were much lower for women. I remember hearing the guys complain when they all found out that women were held to lower standards on body fat ratio, and physical fitness standards while they were expected to run faster, be stronger and trimmer. I knew then I had my work cut out for me, as I wasn't going to just eclipse the women's standards but also transcend the men's as well. And accomplishing this feat didn't come without some grief.

I wanted to excel while at the same time I wanted to just blend in and thrive, but it didn't work that way. In spite of trying to keep to myself, I unintentionally gathered attention as I worked out, running endlessly around the base and swimming laps in the pool. At first I ignored the stares and flirting attempts from sailors my age and rank. But when more senior enlisted sailors made unwanted advances, I saw tough obstacles I would have to face that would test my inner strength to its very core.

But I refused to face the fact that I would never be treated equally or respected by some men no matter how hard I tried. "A" school gave me a small taste of how difficult my life was going to be as a woman surrounded by men, some who were pissed-off they had to compete with me and that I was beating them. As a class leader, I was expected to take charge, and I realized how hard it was, especially when I had one particular sailor in class who refused to listen to me.

One day I directed him to help with clean up; as a response, he sat and made small comments under his breath, describing me as a "fucking bitch."

I ignored him. In fact, I pretended I didn't hear it. But the tall instructor with the soft rolling Louisiana accent obviously heard him because he stopped everything to tear this young sailor apart in front of everyone. The instructor's face turned bright red, and he shouted, "This is a class leader *in your chain of command.* You will respect her as you respect me. She just gave you an order, didn't she?"

The sailor's face, down-turned and red from embarrassment, nodded.

"Well, *what?*" the instructor shouted at him.

"Yes, she did, DC1."

"Well, then, get your ass up and get to work!"

The sailor shuffled out of his chair and shot me an ugly look after the instructor turned his back to us.

Some people refuse to change, and such was the case with this young sailor. Although he was never verbally disobedient, his body language screamed outrage over a small woman beating him in physical fitness, in class, on tests, or at being the first to volunteer for work beyond the usual. He stood around me in silence, his eyes telling me how angry he was to be outrun, outclassed, led, or beaten in any way by a girl. I think he took it as an insult against his ego that he wasn't good enough to beat me. I just wanted to be accepted as one of the guys. I didn't want any negative attention, but there was no changing what was going on here; some men were happy to see me keep up, others were insulted. There was no winning, so I just kept going.

Damage controlmen have a demanding job teaching shipboard firefighting to the entire crew on the ship, and it goes without saying that there are a lot of DC-men in the fleet to meet the demand, but women are only a small percentage. I realized that firsthand as one of a mere handful of females in DC "A" school, amid hundreds of men. The percentage of women to men is even smaller when compared to the population of the entire base, let alone the Navy. I knew I would have to deal with some unwanted comments and attention, but I had no idea that I would actually have to face something far worse.

The biggest shock that changed my life was halfway through school. In "A" school, less than a handful of women had been assigned to firefighting. In my class I was one of three, but the one I remember the most vividly was a really quiet woman about my age.

I'll never forget being at quarters one frigid January morning, and standing next to her. She was upset and quietly sobbing, trying to stand at attention. I knew something bad had happened to her as one instructor gently pulled her out of formation. Finally I asked Chief and he let out a deep sigh, telling me that she had been dragged into a car on base and gang-raped. I could tell he hated telling me this as much as I hated hearing the awful truth. The bubble of security I thought afforded to me because I was part of this Navy community had burst. I was a sailor in the US Navy, but as a woman, I was also a minority on every base and ship in the Navy.

The news of this young woman's rape signaled the beginning of the waking up to a reality that what I'd believed was guaranteed safety was nothing but an illusion. As female sailors, we were trying to swim in a sea surrounded by hungry sharks—in this case sexually-charged men—and to think otherwise was not only insane, it was dangerous and naïve.

Soon after the rape our class was put through mandatory training about sexual harassment and sexual assault, and we listened to long lectures on what should unfold should an unpleasant event occur. The instructors made it sound as if we could count on the Navy to quickly arrest a perpetrator because the victim and her well-being were most important. However, what we witnessed in class with the case of the young woman who had been gang-raped by sailors on base was hardly the example they were feeding us in class. After she reported her ordeal she still graduated with us, but requested a discharge from the Navy. Rumor was that the Navy even messed up her final paperwork—adding insult to injury. That was the last I thought I would hear from her, but our paths would eventually cross again.

Meanwhile, after the rape and sexual assault classes where we were being told to report any unacceptable behavior, the instructors and more senior sailors around us would regale us with sea stories about their time in Thailand, the Philippines, or Australia, and the crazy parties and wild women they encountered. This created an immediate dichotomy: here we were being taught about "unacceptable sexual behaviors" at the same time that the sailor stereotypes of drinking, partying, cussing, and screwing anything that walked in every port were being reinforced. I didn't bother to point out that maybe we were creating our own problems here.

It was in the last couple weeks of school that I finally got around to asking Chief about that trouble that he'd been in that had turned gold chevrons to red.

"It was stupid," he said.

"Try me."

"I was in a room with a door open," he said. "I was talking on the phone and I called a woman I worked with a bitch. She was in the office next to mine and overheard me. She sent a complaint up the chain of command, and that was that."

"You called someone a bitch?" I should have been surprised or offended, I suppose. But weeks after witnessing how the rape of a fellow sailor was handled, and of absorbing under-the-breath abusive comments far worse that this word, I was anything but offended. I was actually surprised that the Navy had administered such a harsh punishment. After all, I'd been called much worse, just hours earlier in fact. "That was the nicest thing I heard said about me, yesterday," I joked.

"Sorry," he said, and laughed. The chief knew I had my hands full in class. And, he knew I never complained either. "You're okay, Strong. I think you'll do just fine in life."

"Thank you, Chief. I certainly hope so."

After weeks of endless information we had finally reached the notorious and infamous sixth week of DC school. This was to be the week during which we'd learn about chemical, biological, and radiological threats, or CBR/D for short.

We learned about nuclear weapons. We learned about radiation, and how to measure and keep track of doses of radiation, which these days is measured in Roentgen equivalent mammal (REM). Then we learned about chemical and biological warfare; we went into depth about G-nerve toxin, VX nerve gas, mustard gas, chlorine gas, and many others. We also had to watch a video on how fast these things could kill you. The video portrayed a goat having a single drop of nerve toxin placed in its eye. Immediately afterward, the poor thing began to convulse and jump, falling over and dying within minutes.

The reality of such horrific creations really quieted us all and still continues to sober me. That humans can write beautiful lines of prose, paint the Sistine Chapel, weave complex strains of music like the Marriage of Figaro out of nothingness, or come up with the Polio vaccine amazes me. But then one person makes something as awful as a nuclear bomb and just screws it up for everyone. And this would be a theme for my life: that I could be an artist and a writer, and walk and talk like a completely normal looking human, and still carry within me some of the ugliest and most horrific secrets a person could carry.

After two long months we were finally about to grasp the reality of graduating and moving out into the fleet. We were given *dream sheets* on which we were to list our top three preferences of orders. Our instructors made a lot of suggestions, and there was one particular instructor who raved about destroyers, especially the new Arleigh Burke Destroyers, as the way to go.

So I filled out my dream sheet and requested, specifically, an Arleigh Burke Destroyer in Everett, Washington. When we all mustered in a classroom to receive the personal orders that would define the next couple years of our lives we discovered that nearly everyone received the exact opposite of what they'd wanted, *except me*. I ended up on an Arleigh Burke destroyer, USS Zevel, and she was headed to nowhere else but Everett, Washington, as it would turn out.

My mentors were ecstatic for me. They all raved that I was getting cake orders as a *plankowner*, which is an old tradition in the Navy where those who help build the ship get to claim a plank from her decks when she's decommissioned many years later, and this was something to be proud of. So, I was on my way first to San Diego to join a *precom* crew and go to a lot of different schools that would teach me how to assist in building and commissioning my new ship.

In spite of my apprehension and massive insecurities, I was actually proud of myself. I had worked hard during those seven months and I remember thinking, *This whole Navy thing isn't so hard after all. Maybe I am just really lucky?* Looking back, I realize how naïve I was. I was like any other sailor in the fleet who was ready to live the adventure.

I didn't know what was truly waiting for me.

# CHAPTER 5

# Irony

On the first of April 2001, I found myself in the middle of San Diego, walking through a hot and crowded airport. My new, starched dress uniform no doubt gave me away as a new sailor. When I stopped to look for directions after crossing the terminal in a sweaty haze, it occurred to me that I was doing all this in warm full dress blues on April Fool's Day, and in hot weather no less.

Earlier in this journey, Chicago had been cold and snowing when I departed, and I was not only wearing my warm dress uniform, but my heavy, wool pea coat too. I was insulated for the sub-arctic conditions. In San Diego, however, this level of dress could lead to heat stroke. The pea coat and dress jacket had to go. I stopped to take off my dress jacket and neatly lay it on a sea bag next my sturdy coat, aware that I had crossed a threshold between two worlds—the letting go of a cold climate for a warmer, more hopeful one, and the shedding of an old life for this new Navy adventure. The sky was a brighter blue than I had ever imagined it would be here in San Diego, and it held so much warmth for me. I smiled as I lifted my chin, and got a tighter grip on the many bags I was carrying with me to my new home.

Along with an overly warm uniform, I had serious luggage: four large sea bags, stacked like stuffed green peppers, two black duffel bags, a uniform bag, and a back pack. I had everything a person needed to survive plus a "kitchen sink" my Gram-mama had joked when she dropped me off at O'Hare earlier. Leaving had been bittersweet; there were so many people who loved me, so many well-worn memories around me since I spent most of my life in Chicago and had taken off and landed at O'Hare many times since I was born.

In boot camp and all through "A" school we were told to go to the USO if we needed a place to relax, or found ourselves in need of help. USOs offer a pleasant place for military members to grab a snack, watch TV, use the Internet, or just put your feet up and relax. They also help guide the new and misdirected, and for this I would always be grateful.

After a short bit of hunting I finally found my way to the USO, and as I walked in a kind lady immediately noticed me. She seemed genuinely happy as she smiled and said warmly, "Welcome! How is everything going today? Do you need any help?"

"Well, I might."

"Do you know where you need to go?" she asked.

"The Navy base."

"Well, there's about a dozen of those."

"Oh man," I said, and felt my heart drop a little. This was going to be harder than I'd thought.

She smiled. "Don't worry, this happens to new folks all the time." I handed over my orders.

She invited me to have a seat and relax while she made a few phone calls. About five minutes later she returned with good news. "Hey Hon, turns out you're supposed to go to 32nd Street Naval Base. We called the base for you and the duty driver is coming in the next hour or so."

I thanked her, and before too long the duty driver was outside waiting. I loaded my bags in the back and climbed in. I was already exhausted but rejoicing a little inside to be on my way to my new home.

As we drove across San Diego I realized what a vibrant place I was in; tall skyscrapers sandwiched by many numerous small neighborhoods, each with their own spice and personality, endless rows of palm trees, homes with bright new paint clashing with fading stucco and whitewashed fences, manicured lawns, and overgrown yards. But beyond it all was the dark blue of the sea, which was why I was here.

We pulled through a gated area, past a guard who waved us by, and I will never forget my first look at 32nd Street Base *dry side* with its old growth trees hanging around like drunken old men. I had lived in many places in my life, but everything about San Diego, from the sight of the palm trees to the smell of the warm sea breeze, stood out sharply in comparison. It was all so surprisingly pleasant, almost homey to me, like everything here had been waiting for me all this time.

But my warm thoughts slightly curdled in my stomach like sour butterflies after I was dropped off in front of a dumpy-looking three-story barracks. The whole place looked like a low-rent tenement, with dozens of huge cockroaches lying dead all over the place, and being tugged around by endless hordes of teeny ants.

But it didn't deter me long. Not even the rundown stairs with cracks and broken concrete could keep me from getting all my things dragged up two flights to find my new room on the third floor. The thought did hit me that I was on this ride for the next five years of my life, and I couldn't help but suddenly feel queasy and excited about the whole proposition.

As I entered my new room I was immediately slapped by hot staleness. I gagged against the heavy mustiness that indicated no one had lived there in some time. In the room were two twin-sized beds, a small table, and a mini fridge. A row of three tall blue lockers separated the beds. Over each bed was a window. I was happy to see that we had a private bathroom with a sink, shower, and toilet with shiny green tile all over. After the communal showers in boot camp and "A" school this was a huge step up. Everything was filthy but that was an easy fix. I made a mental note to get cleaning supplies and scrub, clean, and vacuum this whole place first thing tomorrow. This was my goal: to transform this place into my home.

I pushed the shades back and pulled up the windows to let the sunshine and a nice sea breeze in. Across the base I saw a curious foot bridge over a set of train tracks that was beckoning for exploration. Feeling renewed, I tossed my sea-bags and items on one of the beds and set out to explore the base, soon discovering that the footbridge led to a much larger part of the base, called *wet side*.

I would soon find out what made 32nd Street unique in both the Navy and the world: the dry side, where I found myself living, was the smaller part of the base where the majority of schools and living facilities were and the wet side, a much more massive base, was where the ships were berthed at thirteen piers and was home to various contractor buildings and hangers. Both sides were connected by one long foot bridge that climbed up over a busy road and railroad tracks that had freight trains and faded red trolleys scuttling by underneath. Getting around in San Diego with no car was actually pretty convenient, I would soon discover. But the first few nights I was content to walk around the piers with the slight smell of rotten eggs tainting the enjoyment of the briny sea breeze.

I had been born next to the sea, and I hadn't realized how much I'd missed the smell of salt and the sound of waves washing over rocks. As I looked at all the ships moored in the ports in front of me, I couldn't help but be excited to think of going to sea and getting underway on a ship, *any* ship.

My childhood memories of sailing on a small yacht over Lake Michigan in the cool sunshine were so comforting and vivid that I couldn't help but smile as I went about my walks in the evenings.

Across the bay I could see the Coronado Bridge framed in the red cotton candy firelight of the fading sun, and beyond that, North Island, where all of the biggest ships in the Navy arsenal were berthed. Aircraft carriers were so massive and tall that they could not fit under the bridge like the destroyers, frigates, tankers, and cargo ships going by could, so the piers at North Island were created with deep channels and berths to easily accept their deeper draft. That first night I was disappointed when I discovered a huge blank spot instead of a carrier. I had never seen one before in person. For some reason massive things, things that dwarf me, are most enticing—huge things like trains or ships that throw a bit of scare into me. I found myself looking forward to the carrier's return as I turned around and headed back to the footbridge.

With my first day in the fleet coming to a close alongside the setting sun, I walked back to my barracks in the soft moonlight, happy I was there, and tired from the day's travels and from the long walk exploring both bases. As I settled in bed, I wondered what lay ahead of me; I was expectantly nervous about the next day. When I finally fell asleep, I dreamed about sailing on the open water as a kid.

I got up the next morning at 0600 to iron my dungarees, pressing the military creases front and back as I had been taught to do in boot camp and praised for in "A" school. I pinned my hair up the best I could; it had grown out to that awkward stage where it was too long to be left down and too short to put up. I had to make it look as neat as possible until it was longer, and I looked forward to the days where I could twist it up in a tight bun and look as completely squared-away as the other women I wanted to emulate.

As I left my room I found several shipmates who were also heading to the same ship, and they walked with me over to the building where several pre-commissioning ships in various stages of growth were stationed temporarily.

I walked into the room as a tall, thin woman with deep-set steel blue eyes and brown hair pulled back in a neat bun walked up and stared intently at me. I noticed that along with her perfect military creases starched as straight and even as she stood, there was the small crow with three chevrons standing out on her left arm, indicating she was the 1st class who I was to report to.

She greeted me and paused, giving me time to read the nametag above her left pocket, all while eyeing me for another short pause that was far from empty. The tag read "EM1 Jane Goelid" in a small plain font. She had a lot of energy, but there was a deep running nervousness underneath it.

"My name is Petty Officer Jell-id," she said, emphasizing the soft first letter and short vowel sounds, correcting my pronunciation of her name as if she'd already anticipated me saying "Go-Lid" and wanted to set me straight.

She explained that she was the senior person in my direct chain of command while we were here in San Diego. Our ship was being built in the shipyards in Pascagoula, Mississippi, and she explained that no junior shipmates were permitted down there until move-aboard next year—February 2002. Until then, she said, we were all expected to meet here, and that there would be things to *clean*, as well as computer classes *to do* until schools were ready for us to attend.

Besides her name, she had a peculiar way of stressing certain words like *clean* and *do*, as if this was all she really had on her list for us. I felt her meticulous chilliness, the way she looked at me as if adding up everything I was not doing right, like she had a measuring stick that she was holding next to me, and I was losing points just standing in front of her. I felt immediately self-conscious as she observed me, the look on her face morphing into irritation. Somehow, I could tell she was annoyed and getting ready to say something. This was not starting out well.

She cleared her throat, letting me know she was about to speak again.

"Also Shipmate, I have to inform you that your hair is out of regs," she said crisply. "You need to find a better way to put it up. It is over your collar and cannot just be pinned up anymore. Cut it to regulation or put it all up. Any questions?"

I shook my head, looking at the floor, embarrassed. I had just come from a command where I was an outstanding sailor only to find that the rules were looked at under a much different microscope here. I felt self-conscious realizing I had already made my first mistake and I had not been there five minutes. It wasn't that big of a deal, but I didn't want to stick out or make waves for the wrong reasons. I definitely didn't like being called out in front of everyone else.

She dismissed me to go fix my hair. "Go to the head and rearrange your hair. When you have fixed it, come back, and I will inspect it."

I walked out, my cheeks feeling warm as everyone watched me leave.

In the head I took my hair down and tried to fix it back up the best I can with a mess of rubber bands and two pins. I looked at myself in the mirror, and wondered if this was an omen of things to come. I shrugged off the feeling of queasiness as I washed and dried my hands off, returning to the small room where the 1st class noticed me, her eyes tiny as if she were looking through a microscope. She approached me and nodded approval. "Yes, I think this will work until it is longer. Quarters is about to begin, go line up with the others."

There weren't more than a handful of us shipmates back in those first days, so we gathered in the mornings for the first of many brief, informal Quarters in our working uniforms. We listened to her tell us what was going on that day, and then we were let go to take a seat because there was nothing to do at the moment.

After work, I was excited to explore. I crossed the footbridge and went back over to wet side where I walked the piers in the fading light. I would do this every night after work, until finally I got a thrilling surprise when I looked over at North Island in the distance, and the dark blank spot was now filled with the massive lit-up shape of an aircraft carrier.

What a behemoth it was, too, with white lights on its superstructure that traced the large hull number, seventy-four, so bright it burned spots into my field of vision after I looked away. I stood staring at it in awe for some time. Around me the sun was going down and the air was getting colder, so I finally turned to go back the way I'd come.

# CHAPTER 6

# Life in San Dog, Life at Sea

For the first couple of weeks in the crappy three-story barracks, I had the room all to myself. But one day near the end of April 2001 I returned from jogging to open my door and discovered I'd been assigned a roommate. She was tall with blond hair, and her gear was strewn everywhere.

After the initial ice had been broken we started to get to know each other. Her name was Kelly and she had been born in Washington State as had I, and she was a year older. We had also gone to boot camp and "A" school about the same time. We were both introverts who loved to read and had the same tastes in music. But what we didn't know at the time was that we would later wind up being abused aboard the same ship, and that the horrible way my story would be treated was to set the precedence for her future silence—our stories forever intertwined in more ways than one.

The next day I walked to work with Kelly, as I would do for the next couple months. We both enjoyed the walk across the base, and I will never forget hearing the hummingbirds chirping from their perches, making tiny kissing noises while they defrosted from their torpor as I walked toward the building that our precom was located in.

In those early hours the clouds hung all over threatening bad weather only to suddenly blow away after noon, revealing a sun that poured down light, casting knife-like shadows all over the ground beneath the large trees. San Diego was a pretty cheerful, colorful place, and there was definitely no reason to complain about being bored, even if we stayed on base.

After work, Kelly and I would take a twelve-pack of beer and sit on the foot bridge connecting dry side to wet side, and bask in the warm sun, waiting for trolleys and trains to pass by underneath. When trains would go by just a few feet under us, we would stand as close as we could to the edge of the bridge so we could feel the burning exhaust as they went by under us.

Sitting there echoed memories of my childhood, with my dad taking us kids out to watch trains, which I loved: the gorgeous green and yellow paint of Chicago and Northwestern trains roaring by, the blasts of the SD-40-2s and beat-up, dirty, old GPs answering our waves made our day. Dad would drive us into nearby Elmhurst, Illinois, where we would sit by the tracks on Sunday mornings, eating cinnamon rolls and swigging chocolate milk. We got excited when a freight train came rolling past, the rows of heavy diesel locomotives whining, chugging, and reverberating, thumping everything with the hot power of their 3,000 horsepower engines, and we'd get out and run up to the tracks, not wanting to get too dangerously close, but just enough to feel the vibration in our entire bodies.

But I wasn't eight, or thirteen anymore. Now I was twenty-one. Nothing was so different, and yet a whole lot had changed. Instead of my sisters I had one friend to share memories with, and I was delighted to find she enjoyed watching the trains go by as much as I did. We'd sit on that bridge almost every night after work, quietly passing time, just enjoying the soft fading sun on that bridge, sipping a beer, and chatting about life.

She was curious about the base so I happily showed her around. Down from our barracks by the front gates there was a nice recreation facility and extensive gym and I took her there. The gym was a pleasant surprise with tons of weights and machines to work out on, and I began frequenting this place in preparation for taking my EOD entry test.

We also began riding on the trolley together, taking the blue line into the downtown area where we got off to take the green line to the Gas Lamp district, where we walked to Horton Plaza and ambled around the mall. Sometimes we stayed on the green line to go to Mission Valley to wander around there on the weekends. Sitting on the trolleys we saw the sights of some of the neighborhoods; going under the Coronado Bridge we came into Barrio Logan with its colorful Spanish history and intriguing murals. Then past the marina, where Mission Bay stretched lazily out, and the ocean, a faded azure color, yawned in the distance. I loved the contrast of the buildings, some quiet and old fashioned, old Mission churches, planted deeply next to metal and glass buildings on the water front, and small vessels clustered all over behind them like sea gulls floating in small slips.

We really felt the excitement coming into the downtown area; feeling dwarfed by the magnificent rows of skyscrapers and the constant hustle of business as we passed the convention center and the Embarcadero, where the huge cruise ships berthed, then going past the impressive campus of San Diego State University, where we would get off at the Santa Fe Depot, watching families and kids trying to catch trolleys or waiting for a coming Amtrak train.

We ventured up and down the streets finding Little Italy and Banker's Hill, Balboa Park and Old Town, our eyes taking in everything, intrigued with the old and new feel, the art deco and modern minimalism intertwined. It was food for the senses, a warm soup that soothed my soul to look at. My heart loved San Diego from the first minute, and in that, I was home.

Every day I took my long walk around the piers on wet side, savoring the beautiful San Diego weather and the peaceful views before me. Sometimes Kelly came with me, and we would sit on the first pier, just enjoying the gentle breeze in silence. Some weekends we would go over to Coronado and play in the surf. We had so much fun exploring the base and outside area together, watching trains go by, or watching a movie over on wet side at the theater.

But it was sitting on the piers on wet side where I found myself entranced watching the ships coming and going, longing to go to sea. I was eight or nine the first time I experienced sailing, and we were living outside Chicago. One of my great uncles had a sailboat and my parents used to take our family sailing for the day. I loved the sunny hazy day, the sails, the jibs, the colorful spinnakers spread across the blue sky like sideway parachutes, and the many dozens of small yachts chasing the wind as they raced by.

Everyone made sure we used only the most proper nautical language; there was no bathroom, no floor, no ceiling, and no kitchen. These things were now the head, a deck, the overhead, and the galley. You didn't go "downstairs" you went *below*. I learned starboard from port, and we learned especially fast what *coming about* was and ducked to prevent getting knocked into the sea by the boom when the main sail caught the wind and swung across our small craft and swiftly toward a new direction.

All of these things seemed so miniscule looking back, but they would come back to me with a familiarity akin to going home again: I loved the water, and I loved being underway. Sailing was in my veins, and all this love flooded my entire being the first time I went aboard a US Navy ship.

Near the beginning of May the 1st Classes mustered everyone into a large room and made a formal announcement that a group of junior sailors were going to sea for two weeks on a sister destroyer. When I heard my name read from the list, I wanted to jump up and down and scream. I was finally going to experience what it was like to be a real sailor.

I had all of this in mind as well as the sharp smell of raw sewage and salt water in my nose as I crossed the brow or gangplank of a sister destroyer a couple days later with my sea bag slung over my shoulder. I was both excited and nervous, wondering what to expect, but I was immediately surprised when I ran into someone I hadn't ever expected to see again: the young woman from my "A" school class who had been raped.

She obviously recognized me, too, from her eye contact. She nodded hello in a way that seemed to indicate that any other form of greeting would require a level of energy she no longer possessed. Her eyes remained downcast even as I tried to ask her how she was doing. She shook her head as I tried to ask how she had been, and at one point I tried to gently inquire what had happened to her? She merely said one single statement that chilled me "I was screwed over. That's all." And with that she turned and walked away.

Later, she led me to my rack in the forward berthing that engineering women inhabited. Berthing was a very small space—fifteen feet long by twenty-five feet wide at the most—and home to as many as fifty women. It was an incredible shock realizing how tight everything onboard ship was. No matter how many times you hear this described by a sailor it's not the same as experiencing it yourself. Take the rows of coffin racks stacked three high, the middle rack reserved for shipmates E-5 and above. With a middle or bottom rack you basically have about a foot and a half of space from your pillow to the ceiling of the rack above you. But my rack was the top one, and I realized how good I had it when I could sit up in the overhead and read a book for a short bit before going to sleep.

There is definitely no mystery behind why our racks are called "coffin racks" as the mattress itself pops up with storage underneath. I figured out really fast why we were taught in boot camp how to specifically fold all our items of clothing from white undershirts down to our dress uniforms: you have very limited storage space inside your coffin rack. The racks are such tight, small spaces that some of us with claustrophobia are forced to suffer in silence. I got used to sleeping in such a tight space, and the underway tempo of working, standing watch, and catching a few hours of sleep began right away as I found myself being woken up in the middle of the night for watch.

Underway, I learned I'd be standing watch with the young 3rd class damage controlman or DC3. The DC3 would be standing the basic *sound and security* engineering watch, which wasn't a terribly complicated watch: the engineering watch basically runs all over the ship making sure everything that should be locked is and that all temperature gauges down in the main and auxiliary spaces are within normal ranges. The engineering watch also takes soundings to make sure there is no flooding in the voids below the waterline and checks in at Central Control Station or CCS—the space where all engineering spaces and equipment is overseen, to verify, that yes, everything is as it should be. And as an engineering watch, you do this once an hour for four hours straight.

I was interested in the more advanced watches, and in gulping down everything that was going on down in the main space. Bringing a gas turbine engine online captured my heart's attention forever: I was in love at the first note of the hot whine of 14,000 RPM and it was here that I made my mind up that whatever I had to do, I was going to progress knowledgeably as fast as possible so I could participate in more senior engineering watch standing positions.

But at that moment, I was a DC-man and starting with baby steps. No matter who you were, being on a ship for the first time was a wake-up call because you had to quickly absorb tons of information. The Navy has its own traditions, and its own rules. Some would joke about the *unwritten manual* because sometimes the folks above us would make things up as they went, and we had to pretend to not mind and just do as we were told, *move along*.

One tradition was the playing of jokes on newbies or FNG's (fucking new guys) like I was. And I was about to face it firsthand when DC3 came looking for me as I came back up to Filter Shop after work one day.

"Hey Fireman," he said to me, and in front of others. "I got a job for you."

"What's that?" I said.

"I want you to go down to CCS and ask for the keys to the seachest."

I knew right away that this was a joke. The seachest is merely the seawater intake located down in the main space, and such keys did not exist. Newbie sailors could spend weeks looking and never find them.

So I told him, "Oh sure. And after I get those keys, do you want me to get you a bucket of steam to go with your bulkhead remover?"

He laughed. "Oh I guess you're too smart to pull jokes on, huh?"

"I wasn't born yesterday." And everyone laughed.

A few days into the trip, the CO made a public announcement over the ship's intercom system that the ship was getting ready to fire her large five-inch gun mounted on the forecastle. I briefly went outside the weather decks and had a look around. San Clemente Island lay beyond my sight, and it was a trip to see it for myself, all lonely and barren, no trees or really any signs of life.

When the ship began firing the five-inch shells, it was amazing how much noise and kick those things gave, and it made me ponder how interesting it had to be on those old battleships, when they were launching the equivalent of a Volkswagen Bug out of the sixteen-inch guns on deck. From the flight decks and the helo hangers, to the missile silos that held sea sparrow missiles, I was overwhelmed with amazement and awe at the DDG-51 class and the DDG-79 subclass ships and their highly earned and well-deserved rating as the most survivable and toughest ships in the whole world. This really hit me hard, and gave me some honest admiration for these both beautiful and deadly little ships.

That first time underway was unbelievably pleasant. The better part of two weeks went by like a blur with the ship out doing what we all call "playing in the box," which is a term for sea games with subs and a carrier group perhaps. I think everyone was ready to get back to the shore, although most of these folks were seasoned sailors who were well adjusted to the momentum of life at sea.

As I walked across the quarterdeck I said my farewells with mixed feelings, especially to my old classmate. I was looking forward to finding out about making my EOD dream-job come true, but I had no idea that my career was about to crash far worse than hers had.

# CHAPTER 7

# Fun Time Navy

By mid-May 2001, the pre-com tempo was picking up, and our crew size soon outgrew our little office. We moved our operation down the hall to the larger rooms recently emptied by other pre-com sailors who had moved onto their ship that was being built in Bath, Maine. A bigger crew for us meant we also had more senior people running around, and that meant more 1st classes in charge and calling the shots.

I'd been having dental issues, and so about this time, I was told to report to dental, which was down the street from our office. The X-rays cleared up any confusion: I had four wisdom teeth that would have to be extracted, especially the bottom two which were badly impacted under their neighboring molars. The good news was that I would be completely sedated. The procedure was scheduled for a Friday, and my instructions were to have a personal escort to ensure post-procedure care. That sounded easy enough.

But when I informed my 1st class about the procedure and need for an escort, she became visibly irritated. "Why does anyone have to stop what we are doing to take time out of our incredibly busy day to babysit you while you get teeth pulled?"

Embarrassed by her outburst in front of fellow sailors, I said, "It's not my fault my teeth are fucked up."

"Then get them *un-fucked*!" she said, and stomped off. By now, everyone had stopped what they were doing to quietly and uncomfortably look at me. I felt as if they were reading a sign above my head that read "Shitbag," written in the 1st class's messy handwriting.

But I found an escort, my roommate Kelly, who agreed to wait for me so that I could get the unpleasant tooth-yank ordeal over with. And by Friday that week, I was getting an IV put in my hand as the oral surgeon slowly began to let me slide into a haze of sleep. I vaguely recall Kelly being by my side as I came out of the fog of anesthesia, with the surgeon telling her everything I needed to know to take care of the four new miserable holes in my mouth.

Somehow she got me to our room and took care of me until I woke up some hours later, feverish and feeling like my face had been kicked in, my cheeks puffed up to three times their normal size. She immediately gave me ice cream, and then proceeded to call me a "shipmunk" which was what everyone who had their teeth yanked in boot camp was called due to how swollen their cheeks were.

It hurt to laugh and everything in my mouth was this sharp taste of blood, and the halitosis I smelled coming out almost made me vomit. Kelly told me everything the dentists had told her, then gave me my pain medication, which I gladly took, and slowly ate ice cream as we sat and relaxed.

Monday morning I woke dizzy and in pain and grabbed my light limited duty chit and put it and my pain meds in my backpack to go to work at the precom.

There I was handed orders and told I was to report to my first school. I read the orders and saw the school was for Aqueous Film Forming Foam (AFFF). AFFF is like a strong liquid detergent that is used on the ship to fight fires; it bubbles up and floats on top of oil and neatly smothers a fire. But I'd already learned about this during "A" School. Since I was feeling so ill from the dental surgery, and still healing, I decided to ask the 1st classes for permission to skip the class.

I walked into the office and discovered a new 1st class who asked if he could help me. After I told him who I was, he said he was the one in charge now, and that his last name was Gomer. Not long after, however, the other female 1ˢᵗ class told me that she was the one in charge, and that I still reported to her. This was horribly confusing—two 1ˢᵗ classes competing for control and never, as it would turn out over time, accomplishing anything productive.

So when I asked Gomer if I could opt out of attending this school being I was in pain and on serious pain medication, he asked for my light/limited duty chit, glanced it over, and then denied my request, telling me, instead, to do the best I could. I did an about face, and left for class in a feverish fog.

The class was in a small building across from the pre-com building, so it wasn't a far stumble for me. I was a few minutes late, but after giving the instructor, another 1ˢᵗ class, my chit, he said I was the only other DC-man in the class other than himself. He was a rough and tumble guy with a good sense of humor, and he began giving me friendly crap and pinging DC information off me that I was able to answer correctly even under the influence of pain medication. He jokingly told everyone that if they wanted to cheat, they should look over my shoulder.

I took the only open seat at a table of guys, also noticing that not only was I the only woman in class but the most junior; everyone else had third, second, and first class crows on their right arms.

But soon after the class began, I couldn't fight off the physical effects of the pain medication, and I kept nodding off, occasionally awakened by a jarring shot of pain undefeated by medication. At one point the instructor handed out medium-sized valves that we were told to place in the center of our tables. The leader of the group was automatically the most senior enlisted sitting at each table.

The instructor then grabbed our full and undivided attention by telling us not to do the next step until we were further instructed, stressing, "We are about to proceed shortly with disassembling these valves. They are under extremely high pressure due to a spring coiled up inside, so this is actually a pretty dangerous thing we are about to do. I want *no one* jumping ahead. We will all do this together with the proper tools, reading the damned manual, following it to a 'T' so no one ends up with their teeth in the overhead. I don't think any of us need that headache!"

But the most senior sailor at my table, who was a second-class electrician's mate or EM2, picked up the valve and handed it to me, the most junior-ranking sailor within our group, and said, "Here's this wrench, take the bolts off. Do it now."

Panic filled my mind. "Didn't DC1 just tell us to not do that until we've been instructed?"

He snapped. "Hey! I've been around a time or two! I know what the hell is going on! Just do what you're told!"

I was in pain and obviously not in my right mind, otherwise I would have told him where to stick the valve. This was dangerous business. The pressure under the brass valve cover was horrendous due to a thick-coiled spring inside that was cranked like a huge slinky ready to explode, and I knew this. Surely he knew this, since our instructor had just told everyone, and issued stern warnings not to proceed. When I attempted to remind the EM2 of this he cut me off, ordering me to do it. "Okay, whatever," I said, and I took the wrench he tossed at me. I held the valve, wondering how bad this was going to hurt.

I tried to keep my head away as I loosened the bolts, and, lucky for me—for all of us—the instructor appeared at that moment. When he saw the valve and all the nuts removed, he shouted, "Holy shit! What is going on! Why the hell are you doing this?"

I sighed and pointed to the now shocked 2nd class next to me and said, "He told me to. I told him it wasn't a good idea but he insisted." The instructor turned his full attention to that EM2 and gave him one of the harshest dressing-downs I have ever seen in public. The instructor located the proper tool for easing the pressure off, but he found the cover wouldn't budge. "Okay everyone, stand back!" And with a couple of hard whacks, he shook loose the cover. "You are really lucky," he said to me. "Your teeth should have been in the overhead!"

I may have been in pain that day and out of it, but it was clear even then that the level of danger one sailor with a little authority and a whole heap of impatience could wreak for everyone. I shook my head in disgust. This was my first real taste of an abuse of authority, and it was a bitterness I will never forget.

The next morning at work, Gomer took me aside and told me he was going to have to write me up. I was startled. "Why?" He said it was because I had been sleeping in the AFFF class and had almost injured myself and others because I wasn't paying attention.

"That wasn't what happened," I said. "A more senior person ordered me to do something I knew was unsafe, and when I refused to follow his order, he yelled at me for being disobedient." I reminded him I'd also been on light duty, and should have been in my room asleep. "You told me to do the best I could and I tried to stay awake. I also got a very good grade in the class." My head was spinning from the pain, fever, and lunacy of all of this, because it was soon evident that arguing my case was useless. In the end he wrote me up anyway, along with an infraction for the bikini I was wearing under my dungarees; I was wearing the bikini so I could go straight to the pool after work. No one had said anything about it up to that point. Now Gomer was writing me up for not wearing a full-cup bra under my uniform.

Whether it was from anger over the write-ups or genuine pain, I landed back at the dentist's office. This time, he discovered a significant infection, and after taking it out, he ordered more antibiotics and pain killers, and took no chances—he wrote a chit for sick-in-Quarters that would allow me to remain in my room for a definite amount of time. The dentist and his staff were angry that the command had not allowed me to rest longer, and the dental staff even called to check on me during the next forty-eight hours.

As I lay in bed riddled with pain, doubt, and conflict, I asked myself one big question. *Why had I joined the Navy?* And the clarity of the answer that managed to blare at me through all that fog alarmed me: Because I'd wanted to get into EOD. And I still did, more than I wanted anything else. So while I healed quietly for forty-eight hours, I vowed to recast myself as a steel wall that could shatter any glass ceiling in my life.

# CHAPTER 8

# My Own Summer (Shove it)

After my forty-eight hours of healing, I threw myself back into an everyday non-stop PT routine of running, swimming, and working out as hard and as long as I could. I was allowed to leave work early to go to the pool on base, and looking back, this had probably saved my life. I relished the feeling of everything fading away after I hit the cold water, and its shock that reminded me I was in a different world now; the world of Navy and work and conflict with 1st classes ceased to exist while I was suspended between the weight of water and sun. I would swim rapid laps back and forth, concentrating on being more efficient and faster each time, and to the point of exhaustion after 2,000 meters.

Then I would dry off and jog around base, running a couple of hard miles every day. I had the Deftones or Metallica playing in my portable cd player to keep me company. I'd do pull-ups on the bar in my shower, or down at the gym, along with working out with weights and doing standard push-ups and triangle push-ups. This daily routine distracted me entirely and was excellent therapy toward making my dream come true of getting into EOD. I began to eat a higher protein diet and cut down on my beer intake. I dropped to thirteen percent body fat.

I was ready to take the physical fitness entry test for EOD. I signed up and joined a group of sailors—all men—at the base pool for the test.

First was the 500-meter swim done in continuous side-stroke. We all had fourteen minutes to finish it. I came in at just under nine. I was not faster than the fastest guys, but I held my own and I kept a positive mental attitude. After a quick change and a ten-minute break we headed to the track and PT area to finish.

We had two minutes to complete forty-two regulation pushups: straight back, locked knees, locked elbows on the up, or the pushup didn't count. All of us easily did well over a hundred, going hard and fast until the tester called "time!"

Then we got in position to crank out fifty sit-ups; most of us tirelessly kept going well into the hundreds by the time our two minutes were over. Then we had to do a minimum of six pull-ups. When it was my turn, I jumped up and easily grabbed the bar for thirty pull-ups before the tech was satisfied.

The last part was the 1.5-mile run that we had to complete within twelve minutes. I set off, trotting fast, long strides, keeping the momentum going in spite of my thighs aching and calves screaming. At the end I bolted hard across the line in between the entire group of men, finishing at nine minutes. After a short walk to cool down the techs said we'd all done a good job, and that decisions would be announced in the next week after which we would be scheduled for individual interviews with EOD or SEAL officials.

One week. I was one week and one interview from accomplishing my goal of acceptance into EOD where I'd learn how to dismantle mine fields and set off explosives. And a few days later, I was scheduled to interview with an EOD master chief at the amphibious base on the other side of the Coronado Toll Bridge. This base was across from SEAL beach, and together the two entities are referred to as *Sack Central* because they primarily consist of men who live, train, and work there.

And now here I was, waiting patiently to meet my destiny. The EOD master chief entered the room and shook my hand as he exclaimed cheerfully, "Howdy! I am the Master Blaster here, nice to meet you!" Master Blaster is the nickname earned by those who acquire their Master EOD *Crab* medal after fifteen-plus years of hard learning and service. "Let's see what's going on here," he said as he shuffled through pages quickly, gleaning everything he had to know to expertly draw a quick conclusion.

"You are one outstanding individual across the board," he said. "Your PT and class records are impressive. And you scored very well on the mechanical and mathematics parts of the ASVAB." He went on to tell me that this journey wouldn't be easy, but if I made it through all the schools, I could be sitting in his spot someday.

"Just so you know this program is a critically undermanned rate," he said with all seriousness. This apparently troubled him too. "We are right now seventy-five percent undermanned because there are only about five hundred EOD guys total, with four of them being female. You'll be number five." He told me the whole group was extremely tight-knit, constantly looking out for each other, working as one big team.

As he closed up his long speech he humorously told me that I would have the opportunity to be seen and accepted as just another one of the guys. I would go through dive and bomb schools, then parachute and jump schools, as well as hand-to-hand combat and small arms instruction. Getting a chance to have some fun in the mud, blowing things up, and getting paid to do it was definitely a bonus; I was more excited than ever about EOD.

"It will be a lot of work to get to the top of the mountain of becoming an EOD tech," he said after a number of interview questions. "But you've passed all the tests and are basically accepted and that's where we all start. I've got your back and I will speak to your master chief on your behalf. But you have to send a request chit up the chain-of-command very respectfully requesting to be let go from the ship. I have yet to see a command refuse to let anyone go, but you do need to formally request permission for them to begin the paperwork to transfer you out to us."

As he walked me out he told me again that he had my back, and he told me he would do whatever he had to do to pull strings for me.

The next day I was at work, writing up the proper chit with the most respectful language. I passed the chit up the chain, and settled in for what I'd assumed would be a short wait. After all, Master Blaster was speaking on my behalf to the command. I thought a transfer to EOD was a done deal. I was excited and during the first few days of waiting, asked the 1st class about it, several times, which probably wasn't the best idea with someone as high strung as she was. After her last glaring look I went mum for a couple days.

A week later I finally asked her about it again. This time she didn't hold back. "Gawddamit, Strong! I am tired of this bullshit! Get over here!" And she took me by the arm and walked me down the hall to a large empty room. "You are going to sit in here and stay put. Don't move until I come and get you." And she left me there in that dark, abandoned room.

I sat alone, feeling crushed and publicly embarrassed by the *time-out*. This type of treatment felt senseless, wasteful. She had never taken me aside and lectured about how to improve whatever issues or deficiencies she thought I had, or about how to meet her standards for being a better sailor. I sat there in the dark, filling up the endless time-out with questions I knew I would never be allowed to ask.

Two hours later, my hurting bladder forced an escape from the dark prison. I poked my head out the door and saw her walking past.

"Fireman Strong!" she barked. "What are you doing? I told you to wait till I came to get you!"

"I apologize. I really need to use the head."

By now the hallway was filling up with sailors who, upon hearing this exchange, darted glances from the 1ˢᵗ class to me. From their expressions I could read their wonder over whether she was actually crazy or whether I was actually a dirt bag to warrant such mortifying treatment. Even I was beginning to wonder, which made it all worse. All this mental anguish because I'd asked about the status of my EOD transfer request.

When another week passed without word, I could stand the waiting no longer. I found the 1ˢᵗ class sitting quietly alone at her desk, and decided this was the opportunity to politely inquire about the status of my important EOD transfer request. This time she didn't put me in time-out. Instead, she angrily grumbled about my paperwork having been lost. For a moment I was just stunned, and then my mind crowded with chatter: *When was anyone going to share this information with me? Why didn't anyone tell me?* I subdued the mind chatter and carefully wrote out another EOD transfer request in my best penmanship, and sent this second request up the chain of command, beginning the waiting process all over again.

This conflict with leadership within the command was my first real taste of adversity in the Navy. Everything leading up to this had been inconsequential—a warming-up exercise, if you will. So I buckled down and challenged myself all the harder, running endless miles to stay in shape for the day I would eventually report to EOD. I swam laps every day on the wet side. I ran long hard strides until my skin darkened under the sun, my lungs burned, and my muscles ached. And the next day, stiff and sore, I would stretch and do it again. I had no idea I wasn't going without notice.

A lot of folks began to identify me as "that running gal" because of my chronic jogs over the footbridge, and my races around the EOD building, and then around the first pier past the tugboats, and all the way through the NEX parking lot, across the street by the Rice King and the dry docks. From there I'd run all the way to the last pier and back again, a couple miles one-way. One day I was nearly struck by a car—a blue VW bug. The driver honked and I made out a wave, but I didn't stop long enough to see who it was. If not for all this running, I would have gone mad from the everyday frustrations and the unexplainable delay in my transfer to EOD.

As I ran, memories constantly came to me. One of them included my mom in the background the day I enlisted in the Navy. No smile ever broke across her face that day. I read nothing but pure concern during the moments she softly asked if I was certain about my decision to enlist. She'd been an officer in the Air Force for a few years, and only years later would she reveal the details of surviving her own personal hell. "Are you sure about this?" she'd asked that day—the question bearing a secret note of someone who knows more than she's saying.

I smiled and reassured her. "Mom, I don't have anything to lose. I'll be fine."

I'll never forget that she looked at me as if she had so much to say. Instead, "There is always something to lose. Be careful."

With last goodbyes that day, I was ready to jump off and go on an adventure, go do something crazy. I wanted to travel and find myself in the world. I was running from myself and running to find myself. And finally, in San Diego, I was alone, running to just run. All the while I was trying hard not to go crazy waiting on word of my transfer to EOD.

# CHAPTER 9

# The Sharks Begin Circling

In June 2001, a senior chief, Will Teasle, called me to his cubicle. I nervously reported, wondering, *What have I done?*

He must have noticed my nervousness. "Calm down, shipmate. I am not out to cause you any more trouble. I see a lot of potential in you and I think that you've been dealt a bad hand. So I tell you what I am going to do. Watch this." He pulled out a handful of papers. "These are the chits you got written up for, aren't they?"

I nodded shyly at the chits in his hand that included the trumped up disobedience charge from the classroom on the day I was following orders when I was supposed to be in my room recovering from dental surgery; the chit over wearing a bikini under my dungarees; and a handful of other ridiculous infractions that happen to a young sailor trapped between competing 1st classes. Finally to the senior chief, I said, "Well, that might be them, Senior."

"Guess what?" he said, and pulled a trashcan from under his desk. "They don't exist anymore." He ripped the chits into shreds and let them float down into the can. "Now that that's over with you can relax." Then he declared he was taking me out for dinner and drinks after work.

For a moment I was more stunned by this offer of generosity than by his ripping up the chits. "Are you serious?"

But gratitude turned to something else I couldn't name back then when I felt his hand on my shoulder. "I expect you to meet me at the back gate about 1600, okay?" His tone sounded friendly enough, but I had learned the hard way at a young age that being singled out wasn't always a good thing.

Despite the warning signals going off in my head, I couldn't dismiss the unwritten obligation to join the senior chief for dinner, especially since he'd implied that dinner was a payback for destroying the chits. And frankly, after months of pettiness, I was actually flattered by the senior chief's desire to provide my career with a clean slate, if you will. So the plan was that we would meet at the back gate after work and walk to his favorite hangout, an old Irish bar in nearby National City. I accepted, but I couldn't shake the suspicious rhetoric that was also playing out in the back of my mind.

That evening, we met at the back gate and walked briskly to the bar while he chatted with this easy-going well-rehearsed humor. He was older and slightly obese, with a wide, smooth face that reminded me a touch of Brian Dennehy. He was married with one child, so I couldn't imagine he seriously wanted more than to offer sailorly advice; after all, he was a superior, and we both knew that fraternization led to bad outcomes. I could hear my dad's voice in my head telling me things you never do and lines you never cross.

When we got to the bar, the senior chief ordered drinks and food, and shared his feelings about the command. "I'm getting tired of seeing how the 1st classes treat all of you guys, especially you. I don't like the cutthroat way the one 1st class does things period, and I want you to know I am out for her blood."

"Really, Senior?" I said.

"No, that won't do," he said. "Please call me Will."

I tried a time or two but calling a senior chief by his first name made me uncomfortable. "I want you to know something," he said. "I have an open-door policy and you can feel safe calling me and opening up to me any time you have problems." First, I knew better than to jump the chain of command, so I mentally filed this as his way of being nice. But the way he'd said "opening up to me" had a ring of something inappropriate on another level—a sexual innuendo.

I tried to limit my drinking, but he kept ordering top-shelf drinks. Before we ordered dinner, I was already feeling drunk. When we finally got around to dinner, the senior chief ordered a dipped roast beef sandwich while I took on the house special—a monster plate of corned beef, cabbage, and potatoes. We were both blown away when the bartender set a huge serving plate piled high with food in front of me.

"If you can eat all of that I'll pay for the entire night," he said.

I laughed. "Okay, deal!"

I ate with the entire bar cheering me on, and after a short bit all that remained in front of me was a clean plate. Senior's eyes lit up. "Holy cow, I lost! Where the hell does a gal your size put all that food?"

"My shoes, Senior. Where do you think?"

After several rounds of after-dinner drinks, the senior chief called a taxi and when I tried to pay for my share at the bar as well as the ride home he wouldn't have it. "Put away your money. This is my pleasure. Don't steal the wind from my sails!"

Over the next couple of days he invited me for more drinks, but with each invitation he was making it more obvious that he was toeing the water, seeing how far he could push me, and it felt like déjà vu. There were echoes coming from something almost forgotten in my childhood, because Senior Chief Teasle was apparently swimming in my pool, so to speak, trying to touch the bottom and skillfully stirring up all the long lost sediment. These things began to swirl around me and were soon spinning out of complete control.

He began by flirting shamelessly with me at work, and when he knew or *thought* no one was watching he would aggressively toe the water with suggestive touches and pats to see how far he could go each time. No matter how often I successfully averted an inappropriate hand placement, or quickly and curtly brushed off his successful hand placement or inappropriate comment, he came back with other attempts. Because of his rank, I was tiptoeing myself, wondering how to successfully rewind for a do-over.

After several weeks, he got so drunk one night he could barely walk to the taxi. As we climbed in, his hands began groping me, and his drunken voice and hot breath on my neck insisted I follow him to his room. I knew that even though I had been drinking, I would never go to his room, and I remained quiet during the taxi ride, knowing the second the door was open I would jump and be free.

Once I escaped from the taxi, Senior fell out after me and told me to slow down.

"Senior, I am tired and I want to go to bed," I said over a shoulder, and kept walking.

"Come on to my room, we'll watch some TV, and you can rub my feet."

He had caught up by this point, and he put his arm around me and tried to pull me toward him.

"No, Senior. I can't do this." I pushed him away.

My rejection apparently enraged him and he made one last drunken leap toward me and grabbed me. "You fucking bitch … listen here!"

He certainly had my complete and undivided attention. My mind was screaming, "*Oh shit, he's gonna kill me!*" His anger shot through every inch of my body, and was raw and bright red in the dark night. His strong grip on both of my shoulders rendered me incapable of moving. Suddenly he tripped and dropped his grip on me, and seeing my chance to escape I took it, and ran as fast as I could. I was afraid and running blindly for my life because I could hear him trying to get to his feet for another chase. I left him in the dark where he was still screaming, cussing, and threatening me with unimaginably awful things.

When I reached my room, I locked the door, disconnected my phone, and hopped into bed, shaking under my covers. As I lay there I recalled the one moment in my childhood that had forever, irreparably changed me. It was the day an older adult uncle, who was eighteen or nineteen, took me aside and began inappropriately touching me and compelling me to touch him. This was a terrible thing, but it was what he'd said while molesting me that deeply wounded my young mind the most: *"Don't tell anyone. No one will believe you anyway."* And for some reason at the age of seven, and later eight, I believed him. Or I was too afraid he'd be right. I never told anyone for a long time, and the molestation continued for years. He stole my innocence, my sense of security, and my ability to stand up for myself. But I had stuffed all this down, refusing years afterward to think about the ordeal, or even allow myself to admit it had happened. I thought since the ordeal was over and that uncle could never again hurt me, I had moved on. I hadn't realized until the night I'd escaped the senior chief's abuse that I'd been kidding myself all along. The wounds of childhood abuse may have healed to scars, but the scars were ugly reminders of what I'd endured. So that night in San Diego while shaking under the covers I remembered what my uncle had said, and knew I could never tell anyone what the senior chief had tried to do. After all, I was just a junior sailor with no rank or credibility. Nobody would believe me anyway.

The next morning it took everything I had to get out of bed and face the day, and the senior chief at work. In my throat was an enormous lump; in my stomach, flights of butterflies. I crept into work, looking around corners, paranoid, wondering what was going to happen next. When the senior chief did lay eyes on me, he seemed surprised at first, and then quickly adjusted by walking by me as if I didn't exist. He avoided me throughout the day, which should have made me happy but his avoidance carried the icy undertones of a dangerous iceberg yet to be detected.

Eventually, through his actions, he made it known that he had dropped me from under his protective wing. For rejecting him, the ripped-up disciplinary chits somehow reappeared, making it clear now that he had expected me to sleep with him in return for the favor.

Feelings of anxiety, guilt, and paranoia began to set in. An eerie feeling of premonition overwhelmed me, as if this incident with the senior chief was only the tip of that proverbial iceberg. Whatever was coming, however, I knew that abandoning my commitment to my Navy career, especially to my goal of transferring to EOD, wasn't an option any more than jumping off a roof would be.

So, I avoided the senior chief's path as much as possible within a small command. I kept myself afloat by staying in shape, running every day, and swimming my laps. Studying hard about shipboard parameters on both damage control and the rest of the engineering equipment onboard my new ship provided further distractions.

EOD remained my focus, though I dared not ask the 1st class for an update about the transfer process for fear of being placed in humiliating time-out again. Since weeks had passed after my second transfer request, and EOD was dangerously short of personnel, I was beginning to believe I'd be stuck forever in a command of dysfunction.

But a few days later, the 1st class summoned me to her desk. I sat down in front of her, and she handed me my transfer request paperwork. In red, someone had written *denied*. My request for EOD—after having successfully passed all tests and received endorsements from EOD based on my interview—had been unanimously *denied* all the way up the chain of command. I was in total shock, struck dumb. Then reality struck hard. Not only was I totally denied EOD but I was stuck in this nightmare command for the long-term.

The 1st class cleared her throat. "Listen, your chain of command made it clear to tell you not to bother putting in anymore."

"What? Why not?"

"Because, you are considered 'crucial personnel,' according to the folks in Pascagoula, Mississippi. Anyways that's that, you are now dismissed."

And that was the end of my EOD aspirations. I felt the sky fall in on me that day. Underneath the rubble, I kept hearing the confident words of EOD's Master Blaster: "I have yet to see a command refuse to let anyone go."

Being the first in this case was a distinction I could have lived without. And this was a huge red flag looking back.

# CHAPTER 10

# 9/11: Everything Changes

That September morning, we'd been in the middle of our weekly callisthenic routines when a huge uproar happened. Alarms from all across the base began blaring and people, shouting to one another, were running in all directions. We stopped what we were doing and stood quietly, waiting, looking around and wondering what the hell was going on. And then a sailor running past us shouted the news. "New York City just got hit! Someone bombed the Twin Towers!"

We were in shock, but released to our barracks because the base went into lockdown. We huddled around the television in the common room to watch CNN, and received the news that terrorists had flown our airplanes into the Twin Towers and Pentagon. There we sat, biting our nails, and wondering what all this would mean for our command. Soon the threat level went to DEFCON 4, which meant no one was getting on or off base for four days.

After September 11 things were so different. You could not park within so many yards of any building on base, and when you entered any building you were shaken down and had your purse or bag of any type searched through for anything out of the ordinary. Many of my Navy memories are divided between pre- and post- September 11, and who didn't prefer the calmer, better days, despite our command's dysfunction? But the attack served to reinforce the truth that safety is but an illusion; that even here in our country, on our bases, *anywhere*, something bad could happen. It brought a somber change to life, and so much sadness to come.

But one change we all quietly welcomed was the sudden increase in our command population, because it meant we were getting nearer to leaving the base finally, for a real ship that was closer to getting underway. More sailors began checking in, along with them our new upper chain of command in engineering.

It was the middle of September when I was standing duty at the pre-com building door and checking everyone's personal bags and items. We were in DEFCON something or another—threat levels were always changing—and I was checking IDs and having people take apart their purses, bags, and backpacks to prove they had no weapons or firearms.

It was around noon, the usual time the clouds in San Diego blow away to reveal bright sunlight falling lazily in moving shapes through the branches of the enormous trees overhead. I had quite a line of people in front of me to check, when in walked a new sailor—a tall senior chief with a mustache, flattop, and a smile that hinted he knew something I didn't. When he saw my nametag, he said "Ah, so *you're* Fireman Strong. I have heard quite a *lot* about you." Then he revealed a large toothy smile that actually scared the hell out of me. My mind defaulted to, *"Am I in trouble again?"* I didn't know if one senior chief had already destroyed my reputation, after all. So, I fought to keep a clear face and went on about the work I was doing.

Later he re-introduced himself, telling me that he was Senior Chief Walken, the most senior enlisted sailor in the engineering department. "Strong, I'm sorry," he said about our earlier encounter. "I was just trying to be funny, I didn't mean to scare you." He explained that he'd just come in from the boat in Pascagoula to help figure us all out, and that my chief would be on his way soon. I must have projected the image of a sack of beaten potatoes because he apologized again. "I was just messing with you." But I was still dazed. I felt there was more to this story, and there was.

Turns out, the 1st class had made a point of calling Pascagoula about me, claiming I was a partier and "trouble-maker." But Senior Chief Walken told me that no one cared because I scored well in school and had no other complaints. "Besides, what sailors do after work if they don't get into trouble isn't any of my business."

I was both surprised and sad the 1st class had gone to such lengths to ruin my reputation with my new ship's command, and just as grateful that she hadn't succeeded. I found the bluntness of our new senior chief sincere and refreshing.

But just when I thought Navy life was ironing out, a few weeks later the proverbial shit hit the fan. Senior Chief Walken came into work and formally announced that we had to get ready—Chief Malvado (damage controlman chief) was on his way from Mississippi to get us ready for firefighting training.

And Malvado was to be my chief. I had spoken to Malvado before when he'd called to ask me personally how things were going. Since there's no patience for complaining in the Navy I gave him the standard answer expected of a junior enlisted sailor: "Everything is great, Chief … I'm just living the dream."

On the day of Malvado's arrival, Senior Chief Walken went to go pick him up. We were to wait for the chiefs in our best-pressed dungarees and shined boots. I had no idea what all the fanfare was about. Not even the CO had warranted such special treatment.

We mustered in the conference room, and listened to Senior Chief Walken explain that Malvado had a major hand in helping to build our ship—from the keel up—leaving us with the impression that God's thunder would be following behind the entry of Malvado.

Malvado marched into the conference room with a persona and legend far larger than he physically was. For several moments, he stood in the center of the room, hands on his hips, sizing up each of us under a look of forced intensity. When he did finally address us, he explained that his job was to get us ready for the most important part—the shipboard firefighting that would prepare us for Light-Off Assessment (LOA). LOA was the most critical test of our engineering department that we'd have to pass if we were to get underway on our maiden voyage the following spring.

After dismissal, everyone scattered back to the jobs they'd been doing before Malvado's arrival. Except for me.

"Hey, Strong! Come here!" said Senior Chief. I reported, and the senior chief introduced me to Malvado. "This is your DCFN, Nicole Strong."

I was quickly dismissed and went back to what I was doing; however later, Chief Malvado pulled me aside and told me he wanted to talk to me in private. My heart skipped a couple of beats. I suspected that the 1st class, in an effort to prove her case about me, had manufactured another groundless complaint. So, when I dragged myself into Malvado's office, I was both surprised and scared when, instead of questioning me about attitude or reputation, he provided his number, saying it was okay to call him at his hotel. "We really need to talk about some things," he said, and for a second, I'm certain my heart stopped.

Over the next two days he kept telling me to give him a call, and each time he sounded sterner. I finally gave in and called—partly out of curiosity. *What did he want?* But I shook as I dialed his number. His voice was a hushed, cool tenor.

"It's about time," he said. "I was beginning to think you were afraid of me."

"Why, Chief?"

"Well, I am your Chief. And you have been treated pretty piss poorly by the present chain of command. I know you have been having a hard time here, and I apologize for not coming to help fix things sooner."

I remained silent.

He wasn't finished. "Anyways I am here now," he said, "and I am your chief, and you are my people. I am going to take care of you from here on out, okay?"

"Okay, Chief," I said, not knowing what else to say. I wanted to hope he meant this, and not in a way that would further wreck my life. But I had a bad feeling. The memory of the first senior chief who had assaulted me and then sought to punish me for my rejection of him was still vividly at the forefront of memory.

"Anyways, why don't you come meet me for drinks tomorrow night?" he said. Sensing resistance, he added, "Come on, I'll buy the drinks and we can relax and talk. We have a lot of catching up to do, and it is a much better place to get to know someone than at work. Both of us can be ourselves." And when I didn't answer, he insisted again.

This was a man used to getting his way, *expecting* to get his way. The warning lights were going off in my head. Again, I stopped breathing for several heartbeats; I had been put in this precarious position before by Senior Chief Teasle, and it had not gone well. While Malvado was issuing an invitation for drinks, his tone implied an obligation based on authority and rank. I sat frozen in complete shock, haunted by the memory of Senior Chief Teasle's large hands gripping my shoulders. With Malvado, who outranked them all, this could go even worse for me. Had there been more senior enlisted women in command maybe I would have felt I had more options—a mentor who would have assisted me through the arduous process of reporting sexual assault by a senior enlisted sailor. As it was, the only woman in command that I could have reported Teasle or Malvado to was the 1st class, and given our history, I couldn't trust that she would do anything to help me, even if she believed me. And this brought back the haunting threat from the uncle who had molested me, "No one will believe you anyway." That broke me the most. That no matter what I said to these men, they would either ignore me and take what they wanted anyway, or they would destroy my life completely.

I made some weak excuse to get off the phone, and I sat there, completely at a loss, not knowing what the hell to do. As a chief, this man had the power of life or death over my career, and I did not want to cross him. But I was afraid if I went to meet with him he would want more, and I was not prepared to give that to anyone like him. He looked like he had danced through enough gardens and was an expert at picking lovely flowers. His willingness to use his authority to manipulate junior enlisted sailors like me was rattling every bone in my body.

The next day at work, Malvado pulled me aside and told me he wanted me to come up with firefighting test questions for everyone at the command. And as I accomplished this undertaking, he nodded, as if he seemed to revel in my organization skills and brightness of spirit. Then he allowed me to help teach firefighting to all hands, lead the firefighting teams as the trainer—as well as administer the tests to the command and then grade them afterwards. I took this as a compliment, thinking what a Godsend it was that someone was finally noticing my abilities. And he hadn't once brought up the invitation to drinks or the phone call. I wanted to believe that maybe we'd diverted all that unwanted attention, that things were finally looking up.

For two whole days, Navy life was good. I felt productive, and valued for my work ethic. But on day three I was grading tests beside Chief Malvado when he caught me off guard by quietly turning to me and softly growling, "So, are you going to finally come have drinks with me? We really have to talk." The pressure in his voice was enough to scratch steel. I remember feeling so confused, knowing he was not just *asking*—it was an *obligation*.

I was twenty-two by then, and I had no rank. I was still pretty fresh out of boot camp, and that first chief I had saluted was a vivid memory. But more vivid was Senior Chief Teasle, and how he had tried to take advantage of me and I had wriggled free and run from him only to have my dreams ended and my career side-tracked.

Despite all the classes on harassment and rape, not many men or women in the Navy really felt they could safely lodge a complaint without retribution. Of course, I was too young then to know the statistics of military sexual assault and harassment.

A 2011 report found that women in the US military are more likely to be raped by fellow soldiers than they are to be killed in combat. And it also found that at least twenty-five percent of US military women have been sexually assaulted, and up to eighty percent have been sexually harassed. A study done by the Veterans Affairs medical intakes found the problem much worse: one in four women admitted to sexual harassment and, or, assault. For men it is one in twenty-five.

Back in 2001 there was no safe place to go with this information, so most victims kept silent, too fearful of retaliation—not only from the attacker but also from being labeled a troublemaker by their command. Here's what I did know: I was scared, I didn't know who to trust, and I had no clue how to handle this. Besides, constantly playing in my head was "No one will believe you anyway."

I had no clue how to handle this insistence from this powerful sailor in my chain of command. Each time I declined, Malvado began to up his level of displeasure with a quiet show of coldness. When he thought we were alone, separated from any listening ears by a large cubicle, he became emboldened with his invitation to drinks. I would look down at my work, shrugging off his invitation as if it never happened, or pretending I hadn't heard him. My skin was crawling and my heart was racing, and I'd have to leave the room before my heart gave out altogether. I felt buried alive.

But a man named Dave Gustafson, somehow, was just around the corner of the cubicle one day, and he heard everything. He knew what this was leading up to for a woman like me, and he would later tell me what a cretin the chief was. Dave would stabilize my life and stick up for me, and later testify on my behalf when Captain's Mast would happen a little over a year later.

# CHAPTER 11

# FUBAR

When Chief Malvado didn't get the result he wanted, he changed tactics.

One day, I was sitting quietly, performing my work, when he sat down in the chair next to me and began to work as if nothing had been going on between us. After a few tense-filled moments of silence, he cleared his voice and gently asked if I wanted to get a drink with him after work. "We really need to talk outside of this place," he said, his voice trying too hard to remain soft and pleasant. "Please," he said. "Come meet me. I know a lot of bad things have happened here and I want to get down to the bottom of it."

I remember how heavy the waves of adrenaline and apprehension were as they hit me, nearly knocking me out of my office chair. I realized that my life, my entire military career in fact, was in his hands. And this time, Chief Malvado refused to take no for an answer. "Okay, Chief," I said. "I'll come have a drink with you." His face brightened in an obvious display of victory, and he told me to meet him about six-ish.

After work I got a ride to the Gas Lamp district of downtown San Diego and walked to the hotel. Malvado had said to wait for him in the lobby's bar.

I arrived early, sat at the bar, and had a few drinks to accompany the debate that was raging in my head. I also wanted to scrub vainly at the butterflies in my stomach. I kept telling myself that this was my chief and that I could trust this person, that he surely meant no harm. As it would turn out, I couldn't have been further from the truth.

After twenty minutes I was beginning to wonder if I had the wrong hotel. I was getting up to leave when he finally walked out of an elevator. He looked un-chief-like in a sweater and jeans, and he led me back into the bar, his appearance somehow putting me at ease.

The waiter appeared and asked for our order. Chief picked up my glass and shook it, deciding it was mostly melted ice and water. He set it back down. "We will take two Long Island Ice Teas, top shelf, please," and he threw down a brand new hundred-dollar-bill. The waiter turned around rapidly and made a good show of tossing the bottles around and mixing them gracefully, counting every measure of alcohol like a pro. He set our new drinks in front of us and handed Chief a mess of nicely stacked twenties and a few fives and tens. Chief pushed up a ten as a tip, and the waiter gave a low, warm "Thank you" and went back to wiping down the bar.

The drink was pure bliss. I was actually enjoying myself, because for the next few hours Malvado spoke of nothing but work and Navy life. How he had been entrusted with the sole job of overseeing the ship's progress and how he had been stationed in Hawaii and had been in charge of a large dry dock there, which, he said, was a really big responsibility. So the CO of our ship had been only more than happy to turn the keys over to him. "The CO," Chief said, "is too busy shining his shoes anyway."

Chief continued with his stories, all the while buying us both top-shelf Long Island Ice teas when our glasses ran empty. I suppose he had waited until we were both slightly buzzed before he began sharing more private details about his family; his wife, he said, had become too possessive and cold, like an "old-fashioned ice box with nails glued to the insides." He also told me about his step-daughter who he had helped to raise from a young age and how she struggled with self-esteem, her mom, and boys.

Malvado seemed to sense he'd crossed a line. After what seemed a short thoughtful pause he said, "I want you to know you are *my people* and I want to know the honest truth about how the last six months have been for you. That's why I had to get you away from the Command. I know you've bottled everything up, but you need to tell me the truth. I want you to tell me if anything bad has happened here that I need to know about."

Hesitantly, I shared the details about life at the pre-com. About the daily humiliations I was suffering under the command of the woman 1st class and that despite my outstanding job performance, she had given me a paltry 1.5 out of 5.0 total points, an evaluation that would haunt the rest of my short military career.

Looking back, I think she even knew about Senior Chief Teasle's advances. It was obvious to everyone that he was a player, and that he was trying to favor me with his attention. As we'd all discover later, she was deeply involved in a hidden sexual relationship with him—a discovery made because she'd forgotten to log out of her email one day on a ship where privacy barely exists to begin with. Sailors were shocked to find love letters between her and Teasle. One sailor even copied everything onto a zip drive and hung onto it.

When I look back, I think Chief Malvado was aware of this, because he kept insisting I had not told him everything. "There's more," he said. "I know there's more. Please trust me. Tell me." And maybe he was testing me because he wanted to know how tightly I clung to these secrets.

Finally, I opened up and told him about Senior Chief Teasle. How he had taken me out a couple of times, and gotten angry after I refused to spend the night with him. How Teasle had screamed at me and tried to grab me and how I was afraid the guy was going to kill me in a drunken rage.

Mavaldo's eyes were flashing red by the time I finished. "Listen, you are my people now, and I'll take care of you. That shit won't happen ever again. No one will ever bother you again." He talked nonstop about many things, but one thing he said definitely chilled me to the bone. "You are exactly what I was expecting when I called your "A" school and requested folks for my division. I called and spoke to the master chief personally, and asked for the top females with PT and school scores off the charts. That was you and this other female in your class, except she was set back and sent to another ship."

"Whoa, what?" This was a revelation that blew the hair standing up on my neck off of my body like tiny rockets being shot into outer space. He called my A-School? He knew about the other woman and what had happened to her?

"Yes, I called your "A" school and I got you. And you have exceeded my expectations so far. I am hoping to really see what you are made of in the next few weeks. I intend to get your orders changed so you can come down to Pascagoula in the next month. I want you to help me finish this ship. I need someone I can trust who won't fuck the work up."

I choked, realizing this was so much bigger than I initially thought it was. That this man had personally called my school and requested me, and now here I was, sitting next to him showed me how thought out it all was. And here he was, trying to seem so friendly, buying us both drink after drink. Was this really a huge compliment of my work ethic? Or was there a deeper, darker agenda lurking behind his words? It didn't feel right to me, either way.

By the time I insisted that I'd had enough to drink, it was too late. I was tipsy as a house missing half its supporting timbers. When the waiter announced last call, I realized with horror that it was almost midnight. I moaned. "I just missed the very last trolley back to base."

"Don't worry," Malvado said, "Let's order some food, take our drinks, and go up to my room. I'll get you a cab back a short bit later ..." Even tipsy, I had the sense that he'd done this before.

I resisted, and tried to walk to the bathroom. As I was walking out, stumbling around, I realized that I was so drunk I could barely make a straight line. I vaguely recall the stumble back to the bar, or him saying "Bottoms up," as he handed me my drink. When I tried to walk away, I tripped, almost falling.

Within my mind, red lights were flashing, and even though I was extremely drunk and wanted to run I couldn't. Malvado was steering me by the arm toward an elevator I didn't want to go into. Somewhere in my mind a switch had been thrown pushing me beyond a state of stupor that kept me from fighting back, almost like I was in a conscious state of catatonia.

I refuse to say it was the alcohol that caused me to make this mistake of letting Malvado take me where he wanted me to go. I also will not accept that I deserved anything bad to happen to me because I'd had too much to drink. When I sit in reflection, knowing what I know now after years of therapy, medication, and contemplation of the past, not to mention the years of reading up on the effects of childhood sexual abuse, I see everything so clearly.

I had apparently been walking through life and in my Navy world with an energy that screamed "Victim, use me!" Sadly, energy remnants linger despite all the therapy, because men still approach me today, years later, and attempt to catch me off guard, and I've learned that this is a common dilemma for a lot of sexual trauma survivors. How can we have a somewhat normal life and a job when we cannot control our surroundings or the people around us?

My first experience with a sexual predator as a child had laid a path for other predators to follow. I was not conscious of sexual predator grooming, or how childhood sexual abuse stunts one's self-esteem and emotional growth. What seems terribly understated is the level of long-term trauma suffered by child sex abuse survivors, and what a paved road we appear to be for the deranged individuals who can easily recognize and exploit our weaknesses.

I know with no doubt now that this man knew what he was doing when he took me into his room. He hadn't cared that I'd rushed toward the bathroom and gotten so sick that the entire hotel room smelled horribly of bile, sour milk, Parmesan cheese, and alcohol. Nor did he apparently care when I passed out.

I remember drifting in and out of consciousness. When I came to at one point, he was on top of me, I was completely naked, and he was inside me. I was limp with fear, feeling his hot breath in my face, and my whole mind was a scattered mess like fuzz on a TV set.

The next morning I woke in my room, after just two hours of sleep, barely making it to the toilet in time to vomit again. Lying slumped over the toilet seat, everything from the night before flooded back, and I cried hard into the filthy toilet. This was my life now, a filthy toilet. Did I ask for this? Did I deserve to be raped just because I drank too much? For many years, I would feel as if the rape were my fault.

But what could I do? There was nobody I could trust. The 1st class would write me up, or worse, notify authorities who would question him and believe his version of events. After all, he was the chief. "No one will believe you anyway" echoed in my broken heart. I felt as if I were eight again, being chased around by the uncle who was over eighteen—an overgrown kid, a young man really, but one who knew better. No one thought much of it when he began playing football with me and my little sister in the backyard, playing hide and seek around the house, or basketball in the driveway. He'd play fight with us in front of my parents, and give us good-natured teasing as if to say, "*See? I love my nieces! We're having fun*" that everyone just laughed at and brushed off.

But it all had a dark undertone that seemed to surface more in private, when he began giving me and my sister what he called "tittie-twisters" grabbing us with his strong hands and twisting and squeezing our prepubescent nipples until it hurt and we screamed. Then he started calling us dykes, and tried to get us to kiss each other. We were two confused little girls; the mixed messages were too much for us to understand.

He knew I loved model airplanes, and he told me he had some, as well as model tanks in his room. He invited me up to see them, and as we walked up the stairs my younger sister tried to come along too. He fiercely turned to her and hissed, "No! You can't come! You stay downstairs!" So, she sat on the stairs, dejected, sad, watching as he trooped me up. I remembered seeing her sitting alone as he pushed me inside and closed the door.

In his room he handed me the airplanes and tanks, and I played with them, happily, feeling his nervousness and something else I now know as lust and sexual energy fill the room. I didn't understand at the time what I was feeling, just that it was a blinding fog, and it frightened me; it felt wrong, evil. He went and sat on his bed and shuffled through a magazine, then called me toward him to come stand by him as he turned out the light. He took my tiny, chubby hand and used it to stroke his crotch area.

*"Don't tell anyone. Okay? You better not. No one will believe you anyway,"* he said and finally let me go after ejaculating inside his underwear. And this went on for years. He would go from being the nice uncle, wanting to play games with all of us, to the bad uncle who would find me during a family game of hide-and-seek so he could force his fingers inside me and push my hand down his pants. Of course, I was terrified. Even as a child I knew this behavior was wrong. I also believed my uncle every time he said, "No one will believe you …"

The abuse went on for years until he left for the Army, and then was deployed to Kuwait during the Gulf War for Operations Desert Storm and Desert Shield. After that he would go to Panama and Korea. When he finally returned, I was no longer a child. At thirteen, I was a young woman. Initially I shied away from him, but he seemed to have matured in all the right ways. At times, I wondered if I had even imagined the sexual abuse.

But one day I was drawing a picture of a tyrannosaurus rex when he asked if I wanted to go for a ride with him. By this point, he was engaged to a woman he spent all of his private time with in his room, so I felt safe in going along. We drove toward a previous employer's so he could say hello to folks he hadn't seen in years. On the ride back, he began asking ugly questions.

"So, have the boys begun noticing you?"

I shook my head. At school I was the smallest kid and a bookworm, so I was severely picked on. The guys were noticing me, but only to push me into lockers or throw rocks at me as I ran home.

He purred, "Well they will. Trust me, I can't believe they haven't already. You better be ready for it."

I felt sick as I looked out the window. This was the first time I really remember hating being a short female, and hating my new breasts that stuck out a little more prominent than I wished at that point. I wanted more than anything to be strong and tall, so I could beat the living hell out of this guy, and any other man who tried to take advantage of me.

When we got back home, he invited me upstairs. I shook my head. But he said, "Come on, you want to read a couple comic books right?"

Truth be told, at thirteen, that's *exactly* wanted I wanted: to read comic books. But halfway up the stairs, my palms got sweaty and my legs shaky.

"Well, come on." Inside his room, he produced a pile of a few comics, and motioned for me to sit beside them. I did, but the room began to spin and fill up with the familiar feelings of dread. I pretended not to notice when he began to act awkward, even nervous with the throw of his comic onto the other side of his bed. He lay back on his bed, exploding a sigh through, "Can I bang you?" I jumped to my feet and walked out, half running, almost tripping down the steep carpeted stairs as I stumbled back to real life.

Fast-forward nine years: I am twenty-two. I feel like I am wandering around in another sort of hellish dream, in nonstop déjà vu, lost like I was as a kid, stumbling, trying to run from something I cannot seem to outrun. But I look back and see that the shadows lurking underneath my seemingly idyllic childhood have emerged to try to push me over the ugliest cliff I have ever tried to keep from going over. And here I was again, being caught up at the edge at last, with hands behind me pushing me over.

Later that day Malvado went back to Pascagoula, and I went on early watch at the pre-com building, wondering still what the hell had happened the night before. I felt overwhelming self-hatred and guilt. I had seen Malvado's trap, and had still fallen into it. As far as I was concerned, I deserved my pain.

A week later, Malvado called me in San Diego to say he was working on getting me into the school in Philadelphia that all the senior engineering department were expected to attend the next month. Then he said he was determined to get me down to Pascagoula within the next week or two. This absolutely frightened me; not because I was afraid he could pull it off because I didn't think he could. It was just his fervor, his want that rattled me. Malvado had proven himself aggressive and never-endingly persistent.

About mid-October 2001, three weeks since the assault in Chief Malvado's hotel room, the 1st class called me to her desk. "Your orders have been changed," she said. "Pack your bags. You're leaving Monday, first thing, for Pascagoula."

I stood there stunned, rejoicing inside that I would never have to deal with her again and quickly realizing that I was now facing a whole different beast. The game had changed. I was going from the proverbial frying pan into the bonfire. What I couldn't see coming, of course, was that exactly one year later, I'd be facing Captain's Mast for charges related to the chief among others.

As I checked out of the command for Pascagoula, the chief in charge of all enlisted records voiced his opinion on my new orders. "This is wrong! Your orders read that you should not be leaving until February. Why they are being changed isn't legal. This isn't right at all!" I didn't realize back then that this was a huge no-no, but Malvado apparently didn't care. He had what looked like a valid excuse and the CO had given his approval.

My drinking became steadily worse, even though I hated drinking. I hated this mire I caught in, and I wanted to be out of it more than anything. Other thoughts of committing suicide and going "UA" (unauthorized absence) were never options to me. Looking back, I see now that I wanted to see how this story would end. I was a much stronger person than I realized I was back then, and I was not going to let anyone kill me. So, I had to deal with my messy life as it was, and I found new ways beyond physical training to do so.

When I was off from work I would go walk around the piers, and it sometimes smelled so frigging awful from all the CHT or raw sewage being pumped off the ship—you could catch strong whiffs of it all the way over in our barracks. But that stink was nothing compared to the rampant corruption I would later see going on from the top down within my ship, not just my direct chain of command. It was the perfect metaphor.

Onboard the ship finally, some months later I would come to respect and straight-up avoid anything with the color *gold* on it—the color meant to represent sewage. It would always call to mind the old joke about the golden turd, or a pig in lipstick—how these things were out of place, just as the turmoil in my life was.

My life was constantly in a state of duality, just like the two places I would be stationed. San Diego, California, compared to Everett, Washington, was like comparing the earth to the moon. San Diego almost never saw rain, so it was really dirty all over the place, especially when the homeless urinated on the fronts of downtown buildings. Everett, on the other hand, was so clean because of all the rain.

Looking back, it is ironic that the dirt in my life that had begun in San Diego would come to rest under the rains of Washington State when I finally chose to open my seachest and disgorge the weight of the lies and secrets, once and for all.

# CHAPTER 12

# The Key I Throw Away to Survive

By the start of the last full week in October I had all my earthly belongings packed and ready for my flight to New Orleans, from which I would be picked up and taken to my final destination; Pascagoula.

From New Orleans I vaguely remember the two-hour trip. I vacillated between total numbness and total worry over soon being under the thumb of Chief Malvado. The sunny haze and large Sycamores, fig trees, and comfortable sea-breeze of San Diego had been replaced by a cold, residual wetness, which with the huge drooping live oaks and sagging rooftops of scattered bungalows, made Pascagoula appear like such a perpetually sad and desolate place.

My barracks was a large building standing alone inside a large fenced area, giving it a prison appearance. I checked into the pre-com unit (PCU) office at the shipyard the next day, and began working on ship-associated business. Despite my nerves about Malvado, I still held hope that everything would finally turn out all right for me here.

As of the day I checked in, we had seventy-four sailors assigned to the pre-com unit. To my surprise, one of them was Gomer, the 1st class who wrote me up in San Diego. He shuffled paperwork toward me, and I handled the seeming endless preventative maintenance documents with quiet resignation.

Eventually, of course, my path had to cross Malvado's, and when it did, he kept his distance at first, though allowing himself a head-to-toe ogling of my body. He didn't seem to be interested in making actual contact, and this was a relief.

But the relief was short lived. Every time he moved closer to my paperwork operation, he would stand off to the side and stare, his eyes burning holes in the back of my head.

After a week, our group in engineering boarded a plane for Philadelphia to attend the engineering school Malvado had mentioned in San Diego. When we touched down in Philadelphia, the weather was chilly, but the city was bright with orange and other vivid autumnal hues. After we checked in at the hotel and sorted out the room arrangements, I went to my room first and realized with a lump in my throat that I was sharing a room with the icy 1st Class Jane Goelid. She was resting on one of the two beds watching TV. She greeted me but it had a false and cold undertone, and I knew she couldn't stand my presence anymore than I cared for hers. So, I dropped my things on the other bed and left after grabbing my CD player and headset so that I could tune out the entire world while we waited on the official start of happy hour.

For happy hour, our group of sailors commandeered various tables, and the routine is as you might imagine from the stereotypes of sailors: the goal is to drink every last drop of liquor and to close the bar down. Someone said that the prior ship's engineering crew had succeeded in running the hotel completely out of liquor, so when our group heard this it saw a challenge that had to be won. I was mindful of not wanting to place myself in a position similar to the ones I had already experienced in San Diego with Teasle and Malvado.

But later that night as I was walking back to my room I nearly jumped out of my skin when I turned a corner and nearly ran into Chief Malvado. Had he been looking for me? How else to explain his ability to materialize in a dark hallway of a hotel just as I was wandering back to my room? He pressed his room key into my hand, and in a hushed tone told me I was welcome to hang out in his room any time, like maybe tomorrow, so I could grade tests again. He towered over me, but as he turned, he blended into the hallway shadows so much that if not for the key in my hands I might have imagined the whole thing.

Now I knew there was no controlling or stopping the rockslide that had only picked up speed heading down to the bottom of the endless hillside. My stomach was getting too small for the butterflies tearing around in there. Sure enough, the next day he told me to come to his room after happy hour. As he got up to leave he didn't seem fazed at all that our last hotel room encounter had ended in rape. Instead of following him I drank myself into oblivion and passed out in my room on the bed next to the one my snoring roommate was tucked into.

The two-week engineering school began early on Monday morning, and I remember coming up over this bridge at dawn and seeing the sun come up behind all the ships that were either *moth-balled* (temporarily retired) or, like USS America, being turned into scrap-metal. The ships were casting their monstrous shadows over us as we drove by. I played Radiohead's "Kid A" into the ground. The one song "How to Disappear Completely" was the soundtrack for my life at that point in time. It just added an eerie sensation to the whole situation of my life.

After school that first day was over, I was in the bar, waiting on happy hour. I had a domineering control-freak who wanted our room all to herself, and having no other place to go I retreated to the bar, even while I knew the domineering control-freak who was my chief was about to make an entrance. When Malvado finally arrived, he brazenly walked across the bar and sat down at my table. He made lots of cheery sounding small talk, as if nothing ugly had ever been part of our personal history.

The naïve, young sailor in me could appreciate the extra recognition in front of my peers, and maybe even craved a well-earned compliment or two from our chief—but enough was enough. Once he'd started with the flattery, I couldn't get him to stop without raising suspicion from those around us; according to an unwritten Navy law, sailors don't stand up and walk away from a chief in front of everyone. So, I felt trapped.

Despite years of therapy since my departure from the Navy, looking back can still trigger pain over how young I was and unprepared for the rampant abuses of power. I didn't know who I was at that age, or who I was supposed to be. Life was often about daily survival, period, and I felt like one big Rorschach inkblot. Often those around me who I thought I would like to emulate, or should emulate, would soon reveal themselves as much a train wreck as I felt I was inside. The women and men around me who appeared squared-away and who appeared to garner attention for all the right moves, were mostly walking illusions.

One woman in particular, in Engineering, who worked with gas turbines … despite how hard she physically worked every day, her hair and uniform appeared perfect. As an E-5, she outranked me, and was clearly on the fast track to an impressive career in the Navy. I was so full of envy I almost hated her. What, I wondered, was there about me that attracted such unwanted attention from men like Teasle and Malvado? Fifteen years later, I'd learn that this young woman had been miserable because of the misogyny she'd had to endure from her fellow shipmates. For several reasons, I suppose, we felt we had to carry these injustices as closely guarded secrets. But learning about her story, even fifteen years later, helped me to recognize that I hadn't been the only one singled out for harassment. That perhaps it was time to stop blaming myself for the improper actions of others, especially for the gross abuses of power wielded by those within our command.

Back in the bar in Philadelphia, Malvado finally said, "Are you coming to my room? I have some things for you to do." Issued with the tone of an order, not a request.

"I'll be there in a bit."

When I got there, Malvado was lounging in civilian attire and looking as civilian and relaxed as a guy with a high-and-tight haircut can look. While I graded the tests, he talked, spewing praise over how I was excelling in engineering school. And after the praise, he got up from across the room and sat beside me. When his hands began to touch me, I moved away from him, and he let me finish the work. As soon as I finished the grading, I promptly left his room.

After that, I continued to pour my energy into schoolwork, rapidly memorizing all the info and parameters on the four General Electric LM2500 Gas Turbine Engine Modules (GTMs) which physically and powerfully propel the ship using two high power Main Reduction Gears (MRGs) much like the transmission on a car—taking all the high-speed low-torque and converting it into low-speed high-torque to the tune of roughly 500,000 horsepower altogether. I loved to hear the start of the distinct and wonderful whine of the GTMs.

Feeling the wash of heat and power above me, I got a thrill being down underneath in the bilge, and the guys didn't mind letting me have the keys to the car, so to speak. I was glad to discover something I was finally *allowed* to be good at. And as much as I tried to keep to myself, and blend in, I stood out; I was a short female thumb in a world of very tall, masculine middle fingers.

After class I would go back to the hotel and sit by myself in the bar, waiting for happy hour to start. The idea of going to the room that I had to share with the icy 1st class, Jane Goelid, was too much to handle. But then I had to put up with Malvado coming in to sit with me for a bit. He insisted on letting me know what an amazing job I was doing and how happy he was that he had brought me with him. Oddly enough, both of us had yet to mention the hotel room assault. It was as if the assault never happened. Or maybe that's what the flattery was about: his wish for me to forget, or to dismiss, the assault.

One day at happy hour, Malvado declared that I wouldn't be working for 1st class Gomer anymore.

"He doesn't know his ass from a golf course," Malvado said, and laughed. "From now on, you'll sit at my desk, revising and typing out the 2-Kilo forms to submit to the shipyard to fix everything on the ship that needs fixing or finishing. I need someone who's sharp and has an eye for detail to do this right the first time. And I don't trust anyone but you to get this accomplished."

Admittedly, the idea of focusing on serious work had appeal. But the price? I realized I'd have to cram more dread into an emotional seachest that was buried in the deepest recesses of my heart, and throw away the key. This was the moment, as I look back now: the moment I fully realized that by rearranging even Gomer's life, Malvado was arranging it so that I would have to serve his physical and emotional needs. And I wanted to throw up.

The days, the nights, they all blurred into each other. I woke up each morning hung-over going to school feeling so tired I drank copious amounts of coffee which brought on non-stop head calls. The school day ended with Chief Malvado trying to get me to come help him grade tests, drinking too much, passing out, and starting all over again with a hang-over.

But the elephant in the room named Malvado was getting out of hand. Every day ended with a late-night, less-than-subtle hint for me to drop by his room to grade even more papers, or to do whatever work task he could think up from a stupor. He appeared to want everyone else within earshot of his hotel room requests to recognize that he could wield his authority over me at whatever time—day *or* night. Since no one ever hinted aloud that Malvado was acting in a way inappropriate to his rank, I began to wonder if I was the only one interpreting his hints with nefarious undertones. Still, as long as Malvado was dropping hints and not orders, I considered myself lucky, and safe.

But then Malvado invited me on a tour of the town with his boss, Senior Chief Walken the next day. I was taken aback, but thought that since this invitation included a public venue with another more senior ranking chief, I was safe. I agreed to go. As happy hour wound down to a close he asked if I would drop by his room to grade the tests.

When I arrived at his hotel room, the door was slightly open. I found him sitting on the sofa with his hands over his eyes as if he were in pain. "Are you okay, Chief?"

"No, my wife is going to leave me."

Malvado looked as if he were about to cry. As I reached out a hand for comfort, he grabbed me, pulled me down to him, and kissed me. Then he tore my clothes off, expressing his feelings for me as his hands roughly handled my entire body. While I was trying to scramble away from him, he was lowering his pants, and that's when I saw the shaft of his penis covered with dark black growths. He pushed me back down, and I finally gave in. It was easier to just let him get it over with.

I hated him, and I hated myself. I hated not being able to stand up to him and I constantly felt feeble and worthless even when he was trying to reinflate me with his false flattery. Most of all I hated being an object for him, lying underneath him with his hot breath in my face. What I think is worse than abuse itself are the lies we tell ourselves in order to make it all livable. Such as ... *No one can see what's going on. It's no big deal. Maybe he does care.* Small, innocuous lies, but lies all the same. I knew this was all wrong.

The next morning dawned bright and sunny, which cheerfully scolded my red hung-over eyes as Malvado reminded me at breakfast about the town tour that I'd agreed to go on with him and his boss, Walken. I nodded that I remembered, and after meeting in the lobby we all three set off.

It was a lovely fall day, almost like a watercolor painting with citrus colored trees standing out in vivid hues against a vibrant cerulean sky, and red brick buildings underneath. There was a soft wind that carried a slight chill as it swept up the grounded remains of leaves into swirling masses, gathering the leaves en masse in the corners of stone columns and black cast iron fences along the paths and walkways around the city as we slowly walked along.

Our first tour stop was the World War II submarine *Becuna*, along with the Spanish-American War flagship—the Cruiser *Olympia* (C-6), which is the oldest steel warship afloat in the world. Everything seemed to be normal—two men, either of which could have been my father seemed to be politely escorting me around for a tour of this scenic city. But in fact with every sight we took in the body language and nervous sexual energy coming off the men began to grow to alarming levels.

At one point inside the empty engine room onboard the Olympia it was as if a sudden switch was flipped as Chief Malvado, who had been treating me as if he was a father figure looking out for his junior sailor, suddenly reached out and roughly grabbed me, pulling me into an old coal storage room where he wrapped his hands all over me. He grabbed my ass, fondled my breasts, and tried to push me further into a corner in the room. I felt trapped and frightened because I could hear the shuffle of feet behind us as Senior Chief came walking in. All of a sudden Malvado let me go and walked away, and

I climbed back up to the weather decks where I stayed. I remember a creepy sly smile on Senior Chief's face as he emerged with Chief Malvado.

I tried to pretend nothing had happened as we continued walking around and looking at all the sights, especially the Liberty Bell and Independence Hall where the Constitution and Declaration of Independence had been signed. We were in the midst of everything important to the history of our nation, and it should have been a great day. Except that throughout the whole excursion, I had the feeling that Malvado and Walken had formed some sort of alliance that concerned me.

Later, back at the hotel, I stood on the balcony overlooking the big indoor pond with colorful carp and a small group of cute ducks. I took Malvado's room key from my pocket, wanting to drop it into the pond. If I tossed the key, would I be free from him?

I let it fall from my hand and watched the fall and the key's splash—so tiny that not even the ducks were disturbed.

*If only it were that easy*, I thought. Inside my room, I avoided looking in the mirror. I didn't want to see the pale face staring back at me, a face twisted from the stress and anguish I was carrying from the knowledge that this abuse from Malvado, and anyone else for that matter, couldn't continue. That something would eventually go wrong, very wrong, for me.

Sure enough, a few days later Malvado went on a search for me and asked why I hadn't come to his room. I stuttered through a story about losing his key. He whirled around and walked off, leaving me confused. Soon after, I heard a soft knock on my door. Malvado held out a new key, and said I was to come by his room later. If he noticed my shaking hand during the key transfer, he never mentioned or acknowledged it.

Thankfully, engineering school was over the next day, and we were soon underway with preparations for our return to Pascagoula, where I thought I might be able to reclaim my personal space and life. Before leaving, however, Malvado said, "I'm going to fly back to San Diego to train more fire teams. I wish I could take you with me. But it's best you go back to P-goula with everyone else and I'll call you."

Back in Pascagoula relief flooded me. I was happy to be back home, even though I felt all pent up and restless. I wasn't actually expecting him to call me. So when my phone did ring later that night, I was shocked to find that it was Malvado. How had he gotten my number? As if reading my mind he said he had called the front desk and asked for my room. And why wouldn't they have given it to him? He was, after all, the chief. He said he missed me and would be back in a couple days. I kept the phone call as brief as possible; my roommate was in the next bed listening.

As I hung up she asked who the hell was calling so late and I told her the truth: *some weird guy who had a wrong number.*

# CHAPTER 13

# Up a Creek with No Paddle

The shipyards in Pascagoula were an eye-opener. The walk from the front gate to the ship was only about a half-mile; however, it took forty-five minutes to safely navigate the chaos, and to dodge the many humongous yellow cranes, bobcats, and skid loaders running in all four directions at once.

In a seemingly helter-skelter manner hundreds of tons of parts were strung out, waiting for their turn to be added carefully to the various ships in varied states of construction, from bare keel to almost finished inside the dry dock. Our ship, however, had just been placed in the water after being in dry dock for months.

I'll never forget the first time I laid eyes on my ship. I stood still and looked at her, my spirits soaring. *This* was the promise of the real Navy I'd been awaiting all this time. My eyes drank in the sight of her sharp haze gray paint, the bright contrast of the red paint of the hull divided by the smart black stripe called the boot top where the ship would soon enough meet the sea. I walked onto her weather decks, looking at everything with awe. From on board, the view was amazing. We were so close to USS Cole we could stand on the flight deck, toss a small stone, and hit the sailor standing watch on her forecastle just around the corner from us.

But I was in for a small shock when I stepped inside the skin of the ship and discovered absolute chaos: wires and lights scattered everywhere, the smell of burning hair, and hundreds of construction workers scurrying all over—painting, cutting, welding, yelling. The experience was not at all like the ships I had gotten underway on, with neat white painted bulkheads, and uncluttered, crisp-smelling, and well-lit passageways. Inside my ship, the passageways were dark and creepy, like mine shafts going to unknown places deep inside the skin of the ship. From forward to aft, all bulkheads were a dirty green primer color, and with so much work still ahead I wondered how we were going to finish on time.

Malvado had accompanied me on this first trip, trying to get me used to tracing down everything that needed to be fixed and how to get it taken care of. He told me that all the firefighting hose reels had been welded on wrong, and showed me what to look for. He left me to take care of the first level and then the main deck, while he walked up a ladder well to take care of those areas. I walked around and caught every discrepancy, and then walked carefully down a ladder well onto the main decks where I began logging more. I made my way up port side to find a passageway that took me over to a large repair locker. I poked my head in, and decided it was a nice place to rest for a second. Not five seconds later the door popped open and Malvado burst in. He grabbed me for a kiss, but I pushed his hands off and walked out of the locker.

As I headed down the starboard side of the ship, frazzled, with Malvado in hot pursuit, a large man walking by suddenly intercepted the chief with questions. This was where I met Rich, the shipyard supervisor helping us learn all our engineering watches. Instead of answering anything Malvado just pointed at me and told Rich that he had something to take care of back at the office, but that I was now in charge of some projects as well as training the main space fire team. Then he turned and abruptly left, leaving me standing shell-shocked in the passageway. Rich, as if sensing something had been going on changed the subject. "So have you seen the rest of the ship yet?"

When I shook my head, he led me on a tour, taking me down into the main spaces, asking me questions and looking impressed when I had the right answers. Rich also told me his story: he was recently retired from the Navy after living through a stroke, and had begun working for the shipyard. He was, and still is, one of a handful of the smartest men I have ever met in my life; he had made senior chief in record time, and was a great natural leader, and he remains a close friend to this day.

But even as he became a really good friend, Rich was damn hard on me when it came to quizzing me non-stop on my knowledge of everything down in the *hole*, or main spaces, where I would be working. He brought out my love for my ship, and helped me to develop a deep-rooted respect for the machinery that was now mine. I was now a full-blown *hole snipe*, as sailors in engineering have always been traditionally known in the Navy.

In spite of his tough exterior he had a warm heart, and he was always kind even when he was frustrated. Rich was a firm but caring leader and I could tell he really cared for my well-being because he looked out for me, yet challenged me on my knowledge of the engine spaces. Not once did he attempt to take advantage of me. I couldn't help but wish he had been in the chief's spot instead. Rich was the type of sailor I'd envisioned working for in the Navy when I enlisted.

The longer we worked together, however, the more he began to pick up on the chaos circling my Navy life, and he finally, casually mentioned it over drinks after work. He quietly told me he knew something was wrong with Chief Malvado and the way he acted toward me, and I finally opened up a little to him, to which he shook his head, massively disappointed that this was how senior leadership was treating a subordinate. We didn't speak more about it after this. I knew without his telling me that he couldn't get involved, couldn't say anything, even though I knew he wanted to put a stop to this whole thing. But there were things he could do, and I saw the effort he put into doing them.

From that point on, whenever Malvado insisted on trotting me around the ship for opportunities to inappropriately grab or touch me, Rich was never far behind. It was as if he popped up at just the right time and this frazzled the hell out of Malvado, and saved me from hitting an emotional rock bottom.

People may say, "Well, if he suspected inappropriate behavior, why didn't he report it?" Well, let's say he saw way more than he let on, as did the rest of the shipmates onboard my ship. When our CO himself would later turn out just as corrupt, to whom does anyone report anything? And also, at what point does a person involve himself or herself when they know the outcome will be anything but pleasant especially for the person at the bottom? This is the moral dilemma everyone faced who knew any details about my situation. It was a heavy thing, to know that it was like dealing with a hijacked airplane. The only way to land it was to fight with the malignant person in control and crash the whole deal, potentially killing everyone onboard.

We were coming around the corner into the next year and things began to rapidly change before our eyes. The pace at work began to insanely pick up, and before we all knew it, Christmas 2001 was upon us, and it was time to take off on leave.

I flew home to visit my family and somehow ended up talking my Dad into selling me his truck. He, in turn, talked me into sanding and varnishing every door in his basement, along with all the trim. So I worked hard getting everything a nice Colonial oak color, and after putting a thick clear coat on, Dad gave me the keys to my new truck.

On the last two days of leave I got in my truck to start off bright and early down to Pascagoula. I didn't make it forty miles without having to turn around after what sounded like gunshots going off under the hood. I hadn't owned the truck for more than five minutes when the cylinders began misfiring. I turned around and went back; Mom paid for my flight out of St Louis at the last minute, and Dad assured me he'd fix my truck.

I called down to Mississippi practically hysterical, attempting to reach the person standing duty officer. When you are supposed to report in from leave is a big deal, and big charges lay ahead if you're late, or reported UA. The duty officer assured me he would log in my call, and would have one of the 2nd classes waiting for me when I got off the plane in New Orleans. Relaxed, I got on a plane, and settled in for my flight south.

The whole flight back I tried to strengthen my resolve to avoid Malvado, do my job, and move on. So imagine my shock when I walked out of the airport, and there was Malvado, himself, sitting on a bench, waiting for me. He walked up, smiled, and helped to carry my luggage.

"How the heck are you here?" An appropriate question, I thought, given the duty driver was for E-6 and below, not for the likes of chiefs let alone the one in my chain-of-command. He said the duty driver had to pick up sailors at the airport in Mobile, so he'd elected himself my personal duty driver.

"After all," he said, "you are my people. Let's go."

I numbly followed him. We climbed in the van and drove back to the detachment. He opened up about his feelings for me, and about how he was going to get his own apartment in Everett and he wanted me to stay there with him. I remember looking out the window knowing this hole had no bottom. I didn't say much, and not just because I didn't believe a word this man uttered. I was deathly afraid of revealing the mix of hate and revulsion I had for him. It sounds so unbelievable now to look back and realize I was frightened of this man and the power he had. That he had known what he was going to do to me a year before he did it, and that he might have had a hand in smashing my EOD dreams crossed my mind more than once.

By this time it was well after midnight when he dropped me at my barrack's room, telling me goodnight as he tried to kiss me. I jumped from the van and grabbed my luggage. How delusional and narcissistic was this guy that he couldn't see how much I loathed him? Did he not see how much I shrank from him and tried to escape every time he thought we were alone and he could touch me inappropriately or force himself upon me? It was a fine line I walked, afraid for whatever would happen next, to tolerate him trying to grab or kiss me.

And I hate admitting that I continued to put up with this man's possessive and outrageous behavior and it continued to spiral out of control. A few weeks later, some shipmates named Buck and Henry invited me to go out to New Orleans with them one late afternoon and I happily accepted for the distraction and change of scenery it provided.

Why they call it the "Big Easy" I have no idea, especially since it was over an hour drive from where we lived in Pascagoula. But the roar of the highway, the hot rushing air, the smell of salt in the breeze, and the sound of the guys talking happily and singing along to the radio highlighted the ephemeral happy memories that I can recall from this tense time.

We parked in the old French quarter amidst narrow streets of hundred-year-old Creole cottages and townhouses in bright colors, and walked down to Bourbon Street with its enigmatic entresol houses standing proudly, their prominent mezzanines wrapped with ornate metal railings. In the background loud jazz music played as we walked by crammed cemeteries and large live oaks with moss hanging off them like silken scarves. We walked the lit streets in the golden hour where the sun was just right in the sky to make everything seem long, sad, and lonely. I felt alone even among companions; my deep running secrets created a chasm that I couldn't begin to fill with enough concrete to ever make it solid again. I thought that as long as I pretended to laugh and pipe up now and then with what seemed like normal small talk maybe no one would notice.

But the vivid and loud world around us was a good diversion from my internal conflicts, and so were the good scents in the air. We caught the smell of food grilling and noticed a welcoming bar just down the way. Inside we chose a booth where we sat and ate cheeseburgers medium-rare while watching a college football game, all the while laughing as the two men shared sea stories, all of us guzzling cold beer from tall, brown bottles. We were young sailors having fun, and the night was full of potential.

We finished eating, and Henry took a vote on plans for the night. After walking the streets more and visiting a couple stores, we all decided to haul ass for Biloxi. There we were again in Henry's old Ford Explorer, speeding away on the interstate blasting P!nk's album M!ssundaztood especially the song "Get the Party Started!" the whole way there.

It was at the casinos in Biloxi where Buck taught me the finer points of playing Black Jack, being he had worked as a dealer in a casino prior to his enlistment. It was hilarious fun. We all got drunk for free while Buck showed me how to "Pet the cat" or "Stroke the dog," as he called it, where you either waved toward yourself to take another hit from the dealer, or you waved away, showing you were happy with your hand.

We all made a little money and had a laugh at the expense of folks back on the ship as well. There was this one guy in their workspace they called "Milton" because he looked exactly like the infamous "Red Swingline stapler guy" from the film "Office Space."

Henry filled me on his recent verbal slip. "Oh, he fucking hates being called that too. I accidentally called him that at work the other day and he threw a big fucking tantrum all over the place. I couldn't do anything except run and laugh my ass off." I loved listening to the guys talk. I felt like if I didn't have so many terrible things I was struggling with I could genuinely be friends with them. It was horrible feeling like the icy crevasse I was standing on could collapse any minute, and take me and anyone around me down with it.

The next morning was a harsh awakening as Chief Malvado viciously brought up the night before, jealously demanding, "Where the hell were you last night? I came by the barracks, and knocked on your door. Wondered where the hell you were. No one answered your phone."

When I said I'd been out with some friends, he immediately closed in and hissed, "Oh really? Who?"

I shrugged and walked out of the room. But once inside the head I broke down and sobbed inside a bathroom stall. My life seemed so hopeless and out of control, and yet I knew I somehow had to keep my chin up and eyes down and persevere. Deep inside was the growing sensation that something was about to change. I just hoped it would be for the good.

# CHAPTER 14

# My Luck Begins to Change

The entire ship was called to muster for PT over on the naval base located on Singing River Island across from the shipyards, and it was a long bumpy ride over a causeway to get there.

We had to pair up with someone and a big guy I recognized from the San Diego pre-com walked over and said "Hey! Wanna be my partner?"

"Sure!"

"My name's Dave," he said. Then he curiously peered closer at me. "Hey aren't you the gal who ran all over wetside?"

"Yep, I guess so."

"I almost ran you over once. Glad I finally get to meet you so I can apologize."

We worked out and he chatted up a happy storm. Dave was such an optimistic one, telling me that he had commissioned a couple of ships already, so he knew the drill. Afterward he asked if I needed a ride back to my barracks, and I nodded. I laughed when he introduced me to "Bug-Bug," a gorgeous candy blue 1971 Volkswagen Bug. The scene of his 6'2" and 280 pound-frame climbing into this little car was pretty comical.

"You laugh but this car has big balls. I just dropped a brand-new 1775 cc engine in not six months ago. It's fast and still gets kick-ass gas mileage."

What sealed the deal was when he popped in a CD and the speakers began blasting Megadeth's "Sweating Bullets." For a moment I was back in high school. When I began singing, he hit the brakes. "Holy shit! You know Megadeth?"

"It's my favorite band. I walked to school listening to this tape in my Walkman."

His blue eyes widened. "We're going to get along just fine then!" And he was right, because this was the start of the longest and most loyal friendship in my Navy career.

The next month I received permission to go back to Missouri to retrieve my repaired pickup truck. The drive back was long and tiring, consuming an entire day that I filled with my favorite music such as Train's album *Drops of Jupiter*, because it reminded me of my mom who had said the title song reminded her of me. By this point, I hadn't shared the disappointing details of my Navy career with my mother. I'm not entirely sure why. Perhaps I didn't want to see *I told you so* in her eyes, or perhaps I didn't want to worry her. Perhaps deep down I wasn't prepared for the pushback if, as my uncle had convinced me for years, she wouldn't believe me.

Shortly after returning to Pascagoula, I was told I would be moving out of the barracks into the La Font Inn across town where most of the other shipmates from off the boat were staying, since I had my own vehicle.

I moved into my own room at the La Font Inn, with a nice queen size bed, housekeeping, and no roommate. I had my beloved truck now, so I didn't have to depend on duty-drivers or anyone else. And, Dave lived around the corner from me; we hung out nearly every night in his room where we could unwind with a few beers and a TV.

Dave, at 6'2", towered over me, and reminded me of this working combination of Bill Murray and John Wayne with about 100 pounds more meat on his bones, and a California surfer-boy way of speaking, using the word "dude" constantly. Smash *The Shootist* into *Ghostbusters* at 150 miles an hour and then blend in some Jeff Spicoli from *Fast Times at Ridgemont High* and that's the hilarious, warm nutshell that was quintessential Dave. He possessed such easy-going charisma, and a palpable energy of warmth. He was irresistible, frankly, and our friendship transcended rank or place.

His warm smile and laughing blue eyes told the real story about him, for he was as genuine as anyone I would ever meet. And his hilarious and congenial outlook was contagious. He jokingly called himself an "Enginemate."

"You notice they never put engineering and Boatswain mates in the same berthing, us guys anyway. It's because we'd fuck the whole place up. Those are my brothers, and we've had some good parties with guys in deck division. We're all mates." Dave was always busting jokes, except at work when he was all heart and soul about his job, working endlessly on all the AC's, reefer units, water pumps, diesel engines, low pressure air compressors, and so on.

One evening around the last week in January, Dave asked if I would go with him to pick up some new sailors coming in the next day. The next day he had duty driver, so we got on our blue winter working uniforms called "Johnny Cashes" and were ready to get a bright and early move toward New Orleans. On the drive there he asked me about my dark secret—the horrible situation with the chief. I sat stunned, not knowing what to say. But the tears that began silently falling did. And Dave saw them. He knew what this meant. "I heard him hit on you in San Diego," he said. "I knew that guy was a cretin and a piece of dog shit from the get-go." And with that I began to open up, finally fully spilling my guts and telling someone about a situation I thought was more secret than it really was as it turned out. As I finished up the story, Dave reassured me. "Just stay far away from him, and I'll do what I can to help. And don't worry, I swear that I won't ever say anything. I'll go to the grave with this."

And then he related a similar story that had happened to him. During his junior enlisted years, a female chief in his chain-of-command had taken advantage of him sexually. "It's fucked up, but it happens a lot. There's not a damn thing we can say or do, just keep going forward. Let's drop it for now, though, and put on our fake 'We love our Command' faces, okay?"

That he really understood my situation was a huge relief.

Meanwhile he took it upon himself to take me under his wing and teach me everything he could in engineering and he essentially took over doing what Rich had been doing, which was to shield me from the chief while assuring I became a competent engineer and watch stander. Dave had a natural way of teaching that made every subject interesting and understandable at the same time. But he also stuttered horribly. Waiting on one paragraph from Dave could take ten minutes if you didn't sometimes help him along. And if you didn't know him well, you also couldn't understand a damn thing that came out his mouth. Most people made the mistake of writing him off or severely underestimating him, and he used that to his advantage. But I knew there was so much more to him and I couldn't help but love the dude to death. He became my big brother, my closest friend, and my guardian angel. So I suppose it was inevitable that we fell in love after a time. And though we tried not to tread the sexual water, eventually we couldn't resist diving in together. The closer we got as friends the closer we got in terms of physical space until no more space existed.

I loved him so intimately the details will never fade. I will never forget the lines of his face from years of sun, hard work, and laughter, or the blue-grey of his bright eyes, and how they flashed so intelligently. I loved how his large calloused hands were so gentle with me, as kind as he was at his core. But he was fiery and tough, and could be very gruff and plain mean to people he disliked, and he made it known he disliked my chain of command to their faces. I knew with no doubt that he cared deeply for me, despite certain events in my life.

Dave came up to me, troubled one day. He told me that the shipmates above me in my chain of command were pulling him aside and asking him why he cared for a *shitbag* like me. Why did he care for a *troublemaker* like me? Hearing this saddened me for a minute, but then Dave loudly fixed it. "I then told all of them to 'fuck off' because you are going to be ahead of them on watchstanding qualifications before too long. I see your work ethic versus theirs. Everyone can. Don't let that shit bother you. You don't belong with them." And after work we would go out to Applebee's in Ocean Springs for drinks and dinner.

Dave had one of the most beautiful hearts, and the pride he had in his Navy, and in his job, was overwhelming. And even when he knew about the crap going on with the chief he wasn't daunted. He accepted full on knowing where it would end and he assured me that if I crashed I would not be alone. That gave me the strength to keep going. He didn't save me so much as enabled me to keep walking forward. We met in the middle, and it was the start of one of the closest relationships I've ever had with anyone. There was only one other man in my life who would ever surpass this depth, my future husband, and we wouldn't meet until 2008. Dave would be happy for me and give me his blessing when we would marry in 2012.

Dave and I drove out to New Orleans one weekend and blasted Megadeth, specifically *The World Needs a Hero* as well as *Countdown to Extinction* and *Youthanasia* albums the whole way there, and I remember he had to take a picture of this sign in New Orleans— *Elysian Fields Drive*—which, after I had heard that song half a million times, I understood its importance in his life. As much as that song ranked in his top favorites there was one other that was at the top of his list.

"If I die I want *A Tout Le Monde* played at my funeral, and I don't want anyone to cry for me," he said, in a rare serious mood.

"Dude, you aren't going to die anytime soon. Don't talk that way."

"I ain't joking. Don't cry for me."

"I'll try not to. I promise. But you can't die on me, okay?

"I'll try not to. But my fucking liver's about to divorce me, so I can't promise anything," he laughed.

I didn't want to think of Dave dying, and this moment would later come to haunt me. My heart would be irretrievably broken at the loss of him years later, without warning. He had been my father, my brother, my savior, my guardian, my lover, my best friend in the whole world, and then he was gone as suddenly as he had come. We were inseparable after the first time we met, and nearly everyone respected our relationship.

Nearly everyone. Not, of course, Malvado, who I still had to answer to. And I could sense that my relationship with Dave was reaching a breaking point with that man. Malvado's jealousy was palpable. But I tried to ignore him as I carried on with my work and went on with life.

But Malvado, unfortunately, wasn't the only predator in my world.

One night several of us went into town for karaoke. At the bar was an arrogant senior chief who sailors had nicknamed the *Dark Overlord*, and he was drunk. Soon he was buying drinks for all of us, and saying inappropriate things such as "Drink up, especially you pretty girls" to me and another young woman sailor of the same age and rank as myself. He tried to slow dance with each of us, inappropriately touching us in sneaky ways. He kept buying the drinks and trying to convince the two of us to spend the night in his room.

"You can sleep on the couch if you're too drunk to drive. Don't worry. I won't bother you at all!" Of course, I knew what he had in mind. His biggest mistake was reaching from behind and grabbing both of my breasts.

I grabbed his hands in a strong pinch, forcing my thumbs into that painful pressure point above both of his and shouted, "Get your damn hands off of me. Don't touch me again, okay?" I got his attention as well as that of the whole bar. Everyone stopped to stare at what was going on, and it was then I recognized Rich, the retired senior chief, on the other side of the bar. He waved me over and as I ran across the bar and sat down, shaking, I realized this mess was not only out of control but getting worse.

Part of my job at this point was to process hundreds of 2-Kilo forms from the command to the shipyard to fix major equipment and items on the ship. This was a big deal, because it required sitting down to retype everything to such a level that it basically all but drew a map and pointed to what exactly needed to be fixed. However, it didn't come without its moments of levity.

One day, 1st class Gomer rushed in, hyperventilating about something that demanded priority.

"This is an emergency situation," he said. "You have to stop and take care of this really fast."

With that he handed me a chit, and I stopped typing to read it and humor him. As I read it I thought my eyes were tricking me when I saw the insane *emergency* he had presented to me and I did a double-take before tactfully asking if he was mighty sure about his request.

"Um, you want a deck drain in this space?"

"Correct."

"Um, you know that is the bilge right?"

"Yes," he said. "I am aware of that!"

"You really want a deck drain in the bilge? That's the bottom of the ship, right?"

He shouted, "Yes! I know where this is. I need this done fast."

"Okay," and I took the chit as he ran off.

Shortly afterward, Malvado walked in, and I decided to distract his inappropriate behavior attempts by handing him the chit.

He nearly spewed his coffee. "What the fuck idiot wants a deck drain in a fucking bilge?"

"The usual one in our division, Chief."

"Toss that in the round file," he said, and walked out, shaking his head. Relieved, I threw it away. Even I knew that a hole in the bottom of a ship that is supposed to float was not a good idea. But how the hell a guy who had been in the Navy for more than fourteen years didn't know was beyond me.

It was hard work having to rewrite all these requests to get the shipyard to fix things, but I was a perfectionist. I took my time to do the research and rewrite everything. I would spend eight-plus hours on the boat, interspersed with long hours sitting at a computer fixing 2-Kilo's to submit to the shipyard, as well as other engineering work that needed doing. Then after work, we would end up having to spend another grueling three to four hours tracing out all the engineering systems on the ship with Dave and the other shipmates, and comparing them to the given diagrams.

Everything, and I mean everything, all lube and fuel oil lines, AFFF lines, grey/black sewage lines, LP air lines, all seawater, chill water and fresh water lines, even the ship's whistle had to be traced out to make sure everything was correctly laid out. We were barely getting any sleep, and people were getting to be hell to deal with.

But one thing I did and was most proud of is that I took the dozen pages long test for ERO (Engine Room Operator) and passed, thanks to Dave's tutoring and encouragement. I was not only the very first E-3 and below on the ship to pass, but also the first sailor from repair division to stand a more senior watch standing position in engineering. I was proud. *Everyone* seemed proud and happy for me, slapping me on the back, saying "Good job!" or shaking my hand. When I ran across Dave he had nothing but pride on his face. "You did it! We're going out to celebrate tonight!" And we did later, driving the Bug over to the Casinos in Biloxi. Who could beat free drinks all night? I loved watching Dave kill the night playing Black Jack (petting the cat and stroking the dog), or poker, and I was astounded when we would walk away with a few hundred dollars almost every time.

Afterward, we stopped at the nearby Air Force base package store for cheap vanilla and orange flavored Smirnoff vodkas. Back in the hotel room we were sharing we made drinks mixing the two vodkas with orange soda pop—Dave called them creamsicle drinks one night and it stuck.

I didn't realize it at the time but I had infuriated everyone else in my division. The rest of the DC-men simply wanted to stand fire marshal as all DCs normally do. Now they were all held to my standard in engineering and were expected to qualify for more watches, which was breeding discontent.

# CHAPTER 15

# Moving onto the Ship

In February 2002 we took possession of the ship and began moving everything aboard, which meant *working party*. And those were two words on a long list that I would come to hate, like *reveille-reveille*, *sweepers*, and *field day*, the latter of which means you're spotlessly scrubbing or otherwise cleaning a ship's spaces—and an activity usually ordered when the CO or the XO thinks morale is low, or so the old Navy joke goes.

Meanwhile, work was unending, so we really got irked when Combat and other like divisions finished their workdays at 1600 when the night work was just beginning for engineering. We had a saying in engineering that we were "first on and last off" and this ended up being true the whole time onboard ship, as it normally is for engineering.

I recall that the first trouble that happened on our ship occurred shortly after we all moved onboard. The rumors flew all day while a dozen or so shipmates' names were called over the 1MC or public intercom, and they lined up, first outside the chiefs mess on portside of the ship. Then everyone was sent to line up outside the XO's cabin for what is called XOI where the XO has an inquiry before recommending everyone for the next step. I remember going to find Dave, and the look on his face when he told me what was going on. I had never seen a Captain's Mast before, so he had to explain the process to me. And then he told me what had happened, because I never trusted rumors.

A few weeks earlier, a group of young sailors from deck division had been partying in a 1st class Boatswain mate's room in the hotel we had just moved out of. I know this personally because Dave and I were right there that night. Boats had invited us to hang out with him and his junior sailors, buying the alcohol knowing they were going to drink, but at least they could drink around him so he could make sure they wouldn't get in trouble. We all had a huge party, doing shots and second deck drops where one person stands on ground level and catches alcohol in their mouth poured by someone on the second floor. It was a great time, until an older sailor sexually harassed one of the young women he was hoping to sleep with. I still admire how she told him to go fuck himself.

But this guy was a special kind of dumb. He went straight to the XO and turned over all of deck division for underage drinking. I remember Dave's eyes flashing with a mix of humor, relief, and anger as he told me this. "We're really lucky we got out of this one. But that guy is going to need armed guards." He was right. Boatswain mates are a tough group. They take care of all the hard physical labor painting the outside of the ship and line-handling. They are not the group you want to cross.

So somewhat in shock, we all gathered to watch the first Captain's Mast, and I saw all the unhappiness that follows it. Almost the entire deck division was called on the carpet, including Boats, who stood up and vehemently defended every single one of his junior sailors and took total responsibility for their partying with him. Everyone was given restriction to the ship and extra duty, and all busting-downs of rank were suspended. Perhaps the greatest injustice is that another massive party with underage-drinkers elsewhere the same night had been covered up by the ship's master-at-arms. I learned several huge lessons, however: a good chain of command means everything, and sometimes it isn't what you know but who you know. The most important lesson: Captain's Mast is a witch-hunt. A CO doesn't need anything more than rumors to drag his sailors in there, and he can select what he wants to believe or enforce.

Living on board ship really changed the game when we found ourselves awakened at 4 a.m. for fire drills and *battle-stations*, and main space fire drills. Then onto breakfast, work, lunch, more work. The day dragged on past ten, sometimes past eleven each night. When it appeared that most folks were less than motivated to learn their *underway watch standing positions* as I already had, more *good* news from above: we would be going *port and starboard* until further notice.

I didn't realize what these innocuous sounding words meant until Dave finally explained it to me. His usual easy-goingness was fading. He was becoming more sullen and angry as the days passed. When I nearly ran into him at the bottom of a ladder well to the berthings one day, I asked, "What does port and starboard mean?"

"It means we're all being punished since most of the new junior folks are not learning their watch standing positions. Basically, we will be on duty, stuck on the ship every other day. What a fuck job!"

"So you mean that after all these drills and work and crap we will actually only have a few hours every other day to get away from the ship?"

"Yep. And the crazy part is I got a hundred dollars that says none of this will, of course, apply to the CO and XO." Dave was right.

We went to port and starboard the next day with lots of groans at the shock of only having a few hours every other day to get off the ship. But what really dropped morale was learning the CO was leaving the ship every day. The chasm between Command and crew was growing ever wider. I was single and lived on board the ship anyway, but to folks who had families ashore this was a total mind game. And when we did have those precious few hours off the ship, all we had time to do was hang out in the shipyard's huge parking lots and get trashed. This left us all good and hungover every other morning. You could count on one hand the sailors who were somewhat sober on the job the next day, and even that was a stretch.

It was around this time that things took an even worse dip in morale, for me especially. I was in the parking lot waiting for Dave and the guys, when the most senior enlisted sailor in engineering, Senior Chief Walken, saw me and waved me over to his truck. He popped open his door, and told me to get in and warm myself. It was frigid out so I begrudgingly hopped in. The stomach queasiness began as soon as he began talking in a false cheery tone. "So, Strong, how are things going?"

I nodded against a rising level of panic caused by the smell of his excitement and pheromones filling the cab of the truck. "You know, you really are one of the best workers I've ever had work for me. I keep hearing nothing but amazing things from your chain-of-command about you."

I've never had much of a poker face, so I'm sure he read my surprise. After all, I knew the bottom three-fourths of my command hated me, according to my evals and the way they treated me. I braced for the impact of what I knew was coming. The cheery introduction over, he cleared his throat, paused for a minute, cleared his throat, and then said, "You know, Strong, I really like you," he began. "You are one outstanding gal in every way. I plan to get a hotel room in San Diego, and would like you to hang out with me. I'd love it if you'd come with me, and suck my cock and swallow my cum."

For a second, the words hung in the air of the cab between us, alongside the stories I imagined he'd been told about me from Malvado who had raped me in San Diego. Eventually, I felt the explosion inside my head.

I hopped out of the truck. "Thank you and have a nice night, Senior," as politely as I could muster under fear that he could write me up for insubordination. You didn't dare accuse chiefs or above of being the perverts they were. Doing so would have been the equivalent of dousing yourself in gasoline and lighting a cigarette.

Chiefs, senior chiefs, and master chiefs are gods in the Navy. If it comes down to life or death, and an officer tells you to do something, but a chief tells you to do something else, you damn sure do what the chief says. Except this was sexual harassment and abuse going on here, and it was my word against theirs. I had no rank or credibility, so why would anyone believe me? This mess kept winding itself deeper. Senior would waltz quietly into the engineering office located on starboard side of the ship, and say "Hey, Beautiful!" or some other comment when he thought no one was looking, watching, or within hearing distance. Senior's other favorite pastime was to creep up behind me so quietly it scared the hell out of me when he put his hand on my shoulder, or elsewhere.

On a small ship, like ours, avoiding certain folks was nearly impossible. Many times Senior Chief Walken or Chief Malvado would find *me* wherever I was on the ship and harass me, even as I was busy looking through emails or doing some kind of important work. But the thing that distracted me from everything unpleasant was knowing that after work I could escape with Dave.

But at work I would be engrossed in paperwork or typing out a document, ultimately imagining the end of the day with a beer in my hand, and one of these senior enlisted men would come up from behind and scare the absolute bejeezus out of me. I hated that there was nothing I could really do to stop this. Who hasn't heard a half-dozen or more sad stories about female sailors who had dared to lodge a sexual harassment complaint against a senior enlisted man?

Never had any of us heard of a positive outcome for the female sailor. If my parents, if the public, had any clue about how their daughters—and even some of their sons—were being mistreated within the Navy no one would want their children enlisting.

Meanwhile, the CO would keep the entire ship in port and starboard conditions as long as it took to get everyone motivated. And it worked, because after several weeks everyone hated life enough to learn their positions and work together. But we all heard terrible rumors about USS Cole, which was still parked next to us getting her overhaul and repairs after the attacks on her in 2000. Everyone spoke about how demoralized the whole crew was, and how they were supposedly taking a lot longer to rediscover motivation through the "port and starboard" technique. Morale was pretty much non-existent all over the place, but pain was a pretty good motivator.

Life, the ship's routine, and work seemed tiresome and endless, especially when the inspectors began flunking us almost daily over simple issues, such as lagging (insulation on piping and valves). But I climbed down in the hole with the rest of the sailors to fix it. We would fan out and work hard, re-doing stuff, only to re-do it all again the next day to another's even higher standard. The other men accepted me as one of their own, and were grateful for whatever help I gave them.

I cannot tell you how much this finally meant to find a place that I fit into. During my entire Navy experience, I'd always worked hard and to the best of my ability. Hadn't I proven this over and over again with my physical fitness tests, the EOD rigorous qualifications I'd passed, and qualifying for a more senior watch in engineering? To some I might have appeared more motivated or intelligent. Truth is, I just had more to prove—to myself, to everyone. I was driven to prove that I was so much more than the rumors that were encircling me.

In that moment, I knew then I wanted to become a gas turbine tech (GSM), or an engineman (EN), like Dave. Besides loving all the equipment down in the hole, I loved working with the sailors in both chains-of-command, and they treated me well; the majority of them did, at least. I had to deal with one or two who didn't like competing with a *girl* just as I had in "A" school. But the Navy, despite its problems with poor senior leadership and abuses of power, had taught me something about myself that I probably never would have known otherwise—I was rather mechanically inclined.

To block out work stress and kill time, Dave and I would get a room together on the weekends, where we would watch TV, play video games, drink, and relax. In a sense, we lived as partners, as a husband and wife would live—right down to doing our laundry together. And at the hotel we quickly realized we weren't the only men and women shipmates pairing up and doing so; a whole lot of other shipmates were quietly partying together as well. Some would be sneaking out of rooms to go to other ones when they thought no one saw them.

Back on the ship it seemed as if everyone was going crazy, talking about who they thought was screwing whom, or who would be screwing whom next. This was back before smart phones or social media, thank goodness. Gossip among the men was actually the worst. I had no idea until years later what an ugly reputation I actually had. One of my friends finally shared that a sailor had asked if I "took it in the ass," and my friend said it had taken great control not to throat punch the sailor. But I wasn't the only woman sailor discussed in such ways. Every woman was, according to my friend.

So it was no surprise when everyone on the ship knew that a couple of junior and senior officers were sexually active with enlisted sailors. This level of fraternization was considered a huge offense, and an indicator of a much bigger problem onboard our ship. Soon word spread throughout the ship that higher-ranking officers were entertaining young women on and off the ship, and giving *tours of the ship* during odd hours. The sailors standing watch as officer of the deck (OOD) on the Quarterdeck, witnessed the debauchery that was happening during their four-hour watch and had to pretend they hadn't, however disgusting or painful the memory.

And being married was anything but a deterrent, as I'd firsthand discovered by the chiefs who had assaulted me and continued to harass me. In my own division, it was obvious a senior leader was entangled in an intimate hook-up with a blond shipmate, erstwhile his pregnant wife at home was due to deliver any day.

A lot of fellow shipmates hooked-up with someone, which I understood. The advantage for most women shipmates, myself included, was to engage in a relationship that would hopefully ward off all the other unwanted sexual attention.

What never made sense to me living and trying to survive in this pressure cooker environment was that anyone thought that throwing men and women on top of each other *wouldn't* naturally lead to sexual relationships. Add to this the abuses of power that stemmed from the top down to senior enlisted and you have an idea of how out of control the mess on board my ship was.

Not that everything was all dark and negative. I met good sailors—men and women who never caused trouble. And there were plenty of situations that made life worth looking forward to, like daily mail call. My dad had recently called and told me that he was sending a gift in the mail. Not knowing what to expect I went up to wait outside the ship's post office, waiting in a long line with everyone else.

After the first week of hearing I had nothing, Don Carrel, the postmaster finally announced, "Hey Strong, I got a big package for you!" Hearing this brightened my day, wondering what was in store for me. He happily presented a large box, and I walked away, my arms heavy as I clutched my cardboard surprise. I opened it and found a large carrying case containing an Olympus SLR film camera and lenses of several sizes. This gift, so unexpected, meant so much. I still had my parents' support, and Dave's. My dark world was not

so terribly blackened by the constant sexual harassment and game playing that I woul
up hope, *yet*. I put the camera safely in my rack and locked it up, my heart filling up wi
for the unknown storms that lay ahead.

# CHAPTER 16

# A Different Perspective

Back in our ship's post office, Don Carrel, the postmaster, finished handing out the last of the mail, eager to be on his way, although reluctant to take over his responsibilities that evening as duty driver. Duty driver was a twenty-four hour watch that meant dealing with various repetitive situations, and some would prove more unpredictable than others. Don was a pretty easygoing fellow with a sense of humor as bright as his blue eyes; he was tall, but as a shy-natured man he was able to blend in well, which suited him. His was the job of handling and sorting all mail brought to the ship, and then handing it out, which meant he was one of the few people who came into contact with every single member of our ship's 300-person crew ranging from every junior enlisted, to chiefs, officers, and the commanding officer himself. Don saw everything and rarely spoke about anything, which gave him the ability to blend seamlessly into the background and almost be forgotten.

Don told me later that he always wondered what the day had in store whenever he assumed the watch for duty driver because one never knew what to expect. Mostly he picked up shipmates from the airport, but once in a while he had the drunk and belligerent shipmate who would give him a hard time. But that night as he got in the white van and put the key in the ignition he had no idea what a ride he was in for.

The first part of the watch that evening was pretty uneventful. But just as he was thinking he was free, the cell phone rang. The caller was the command master chief, requesting a pick-up at the bar in Gautier. "I'll be right there, Master Chief," he said. Don drove to the bar, telling me later he walked in to find a large crowd of people scattered all over, among them several top-ranking officers on the ship, including one the crew had nicknamed

"Captain Redlight" because of his notoriety for philandering with young women on and off the ship. Tonight was obviously no different; Don saw Captain Redlight with a young woman who seemed to have interest in more than Redlight's conversation.

Don noticed the command master chief at the same moment the master chief recognized and waved him over. "Crazy night?"

"I think I'm almost ready to go," the master chief said. "Let me finish this drink."

"No problem," Don said, and ordered a Coke.

Just then Captain Redlight, drunk, stumbled to the bar with his lady friend and fell when he tried to perch atop a barstool. His friend helped him to his feet, and he loudly ordered drinks for the two of them. "I am an officer in the Navy," he said to the woman, and for Don and all to hear.

"Really?" she said.

"Yep. The commander of a mighty destroyer. You should come visit sometime. I'll give you a tour on board her."

"That sounds like fun," she said.

As the CO began to describe the things he planned to show her, including his stateroom, Don cleared his throat, as did the command master chief—both looking uncomfortably at one another with the realization they needed to leave before they heard too much from this captain, who was married. Don regularly handled the CO's mail and knew every time the man's wife sent a letter.

The master chief and several other sailors followed Don to the van in the parking lot. Everyone found a seat and a seatbelt. Just as Don was about to pull away, Captain Redlight appeared, knocking on a window. "Hey, I need a ride. Someone slashed the tires on my car."

"Okay, Sir," Don said. "Climb in." The captain walked around and clumsily opened the passenger door where the master chief was sitting.

"I need this seat in case I'm sick." The master chief patiently climbed out of the passenger seat, and into the back.

Don said he was already on the interstate when he noticed the flashing of red and blue lights in the rear-view mirror. A state trooper pulled alongside the van and signaled for Don to pull over. He said his stomach flipped like a pancake.

In the passenger seat Captain Redlight was growing agitated, and Don hoped that the stop would be quick. But the state trooper was deliberately slow in his approach of the van. Don lowered his window for the trooper, and let in the roar of interstate traffic.

The trooper, Don said, spoke through a heavy southern drawl. "Good evening, boys. The reason I pulled you all over was to inform you that your brake lights are out." The trooper had bent low toward Don to speak over the loud rush of traffic. This was when Captain Redlight, seated in the front passenger seat, shouted, "You are only bothering us because I am black." Don said he caught the expressions of shock in his rear-view mirror. The surprised trooper, said, "Excuse me, boy?"

Captain Redlight had light brown skin, but that was beside the point. The captain kept shouting at the trooper and wanted to fight. Fortunately, the master chief jumped in to calm the skipper. "Now, Sir, you know this is just a routine stop, we've all partied a little bit too much tonight, and no need to give this officer doing his job a hard time."

Don would tell me later that he'd apologized to the trooper and explained that everyone in the van was drunk and his job was to get everyone safely back to the ship. The trooper looked carefully at each sailor for what seemed far too long, and finally issued Don a warning.

"I apologize again for bothering you guys. Have a good night. Get those brake lights fixed and drive safely."

"Yes, sir. I will." Don said as he rolled up the window up, happy to have this situation almost over with. What he didn't know was that it would not be the last time this ship's commander would present a problem. Soon the sea stories from shipmates about this captain included antics of used condoms or women's underwear discovered on the floor in his stateroom.

This particular man and his hypocrisy would indeed leave a horrible, long-lasting impression in the mouths of the majority of our crew who served underneath him. That he was himself a married man who chased after young women and brought them on and off the ship, giving direct orders to the shipmate's standing watch to specifically not log in his guests, were egregious infractions of the rules of good conduct and order. That he did this showed he held himself to a different rule altogether, and it was obvious he existed to serve himself and not the needs of his ship or crew, and this would never be forgotten by anyone.

No one would forget his bitter, self-serving legacy, especially not the people he would humiliate before the entire command in the coming months when a large scandal and charges of rape and sexual harassment became public.

# CHAPTER 17

# Panama Canal

In April 2002 we were ready to undergo light-off assessment (LOA). This was the biggest test of our new engineering team during which we had to prove that we could pull together as a team to get the gas turbine engines and everything else in the main spaces running smoothly, as well as handle an emergency situation.

During the actual test we not only had to man our underway watch standing positions but handle battle stations when a make-up fire casualty was called. So far our crew had performed to satisfaction, working well together to fire up the propulsion and electrical systems in the main spaces. Now we had to prove we could fight a fire.

I was put in charge of training the team that consisted of brand-new junior sailors. I realized most of them could barely swim, and that meant they were motivated to put out any fire to keep the ship afloat. I capitalized on this, and soon we were all up every day before dawn, running drills, standing around for the better part of two to three hours a day in stuffy ski-suit like fire gear, with heavy scuba tanks on our backs and full-face masks that made me claustrophobic, but I kept going. Eventually, the team could dress in full gear and scramble in place in less than five minutes.

During one of these critical engineering tests, however, we came close to an actual catastrophe. We were performing what seemed like a simple fuel-oil transfer. Suddenly hundreds of gallons of fuel oil went spilling into the bilges through an open valve, filling the bilges and causing everyone to panic. This was a real, large emergency, and my main space fire team and I sprang into action by dressing and rushing down into the main space within minutes of the alarm. We discovered chaos—fuel sloshing everywhere and it stung our eyes to see. As soon as we secured everything, we prepared for cleanup. We knew the whole ship had failed its test, but the mess still had to be dealt with.

The situation worsened when the officer-in-charge of engineering lost composure in front of the entire command. He threw his paperwork over his head and burst in tears. "But I wasn't trained for this!" For a while, no one spoke. We stood around him in stunned silence, because the vast majority of us had worked and trained hard for this test. We had busted our butts to get the ship to this point only to witness our OIC's meltdown over a single mishap.

But somehow, and I don't understand how or why, we received a pass on the inspection. Maybe the inspectors in charge felt sorry for us. It might very well have been the responsiveness of our outstanding fire team to get there within mere minutes to secure the site that had impressed them. Whatever the reason, we all had one hell of a party afterward in the parking lots.

By the time we'd passed the final test it was mid-April, and we were ready to get underway on our voyage to the Panama Canal. We waved goodbye, and I was soaking in the hazy sun when five minutes into our maiden voyage, I was delivered the news that I was being sent to the galley and mess decks to do my time in the galley. Everyone in the Navy who's enlisted has to serve three months in the galley doing what's called *mess-cranking*. Apparently, it was my turn for mess cranking.

I knew I was in trouble when the *Dark Overlord* handed over a toothbrush and a bucket, and ordered me to scrub the mess line—a space roughly sixty feet long by five feet wide. "All of it," he said. As I got down on my knees to begin this backbreaking labor I knew this was payback for the humiliation I'd caused him months earlier after he publicly grabbed my breasts. I scrubbed hard and pulled up a ton of dirt that had accumulated in the ridges of the non-skid. I wasn't going to half-ass the job merely because it was given to me out of spite.

After about two weeks the deck was finished, so I was sent to the deep sink. Everyone dreads the deep sink. You have to wash all the endless galley cookware in a sink that's large enough to take a whirlpool bath in and with water hot enough to induce third-degree burns by the steam alone. The deep sink is hard manual labor that most sailors want nothing to do with. But after scrubbing the deck with a toothbrush for more than twelve hours a day, duty at the deep sink was heaven. Deep sink was the one place no one bothered me; the cooks left me alone, and I never had to serve food. The biggest perk—no chief or senior chief would ever think of bothering me during Deep Sink.

So I spent a huge amount of my day singing to myself, meditating, or laughing at the Filipino mess cook who made fun of the chiefs in their private "chief's mess" next to the galley. The cook thought they were too soft, fat, and whiny. He was a nice guy who would talk in his quiet accent and tell stories about the chiefs who came back for very large seconds, thirds, even fourth servings at every meal. The way he said, "Dos mudder puckers" was hilarious. He would shake his head in disgust and we would laugh, knowing exactly who he was talking about: the same overweight chiefs, who, when finished with their myocardial infarction inducing portions, admonished the enlisted sailors about weight-standards.

Within a week or two it was announced that we were getting ready to traverse the Panama Canal. Everyone looked for an excuse to be outside the skin of the ship for a view of the world around us. After my Deep Sink work was finished, I went above deck too. All around us, hundreds of huge oil tankers and cargo ships were anchored, waiting their turn to go through the canal. Our ship had permission to cut in line.

I remember vividly that it was around nine when the call went out to prepare for our transit into the first set of locks. We all went topside to a night full of intrusive blinding lights and ancient crumbling canal—a surreal juxtaposition against darkness, lush tropical humidity, and canal operators who were yelling, what some sailors recognized as cursing, in a foreign language.

I needed to pinch myself it was all so unbelievable. We were finally going through Teddy Roosevelt's own masterpiece of innovation, under a warm torrential downpour as if God had turned on a bath faucet. We were all thankful for the rain; it was a chance to escape a little sludge. Several sailors actually took a full-shower or washed their armpits with the rain. We danced around and acted goofy, catching the sweet rain on our tongues, and praying for it to rain harder, and it did. All crankers and mess cooks were off duty two hours afterward, so we went back up to the weather decks to clean ourselves again in the downpour.

A little later that night I went up to visit my friend, Spook, who was standing watch on the portside .50 caliber gun above the breezeway. By this time we were in the middle of Lake Gatun heading toward the last set of locks and the Pacific Ocean. Moonlight bounced like a dark, flat stone off the water. I thought it was so lovely and got dreamily lost in the poetic beauty of the moment. I asked Spook how he felt at this point in time, and he said scared-shitless.

"Why's that?" I asked.

He told me something I didn't want to know. "Well, we are basically helpless in the middle of this third-world country if shit decided to hit the fan."

I stood there and realized he was right. We were on a new ship and nothing worked, and even if it did we had no projectiles for the five-inch gun, let alone missiles in our cells forward and back aft to shoot off.

"All we really have to protect us are small arms and the .50 cal guns. We have not been fitted with *Seawhizz* yet. But in a big pinch we could use the Aegis radar, and the electromagnetic pulse would black shit out for a good couple-mile radius." Now I was feeling spooked but he wasn't finished. "It might stop the rat bastards trying to mess with us, sure, but the downside being that the two of us and whoever else was outside the skin of the ship would ultimately be rendered childless, most specifically us being we are standing in the Aegis hotspot under the 'DANGER! Microwaves!' sign."

I felt a tad less enchanted with the whole evening as I headed back inside the skin of the ship for my rack. I counted sheep until the *Mess-Cook-Mess-Crank* wakeup at 0430.

I woke early to find the ship stilled, in port at an old US Navy base outside the last set of locks. We had given this base to Panama, and I could see why when we took trash outside to dump it one last time before we got underway at 0600: it wasn't the port with the nicest view. The place was one big hovel, a sweaty desolate collection of fading yellow and white painted cinderblock buildings crumbling as the jungle took back control. I lingered a bit above deck, getting a fresh breath before having to resume my work.

A few hours later when we were underway toward the Pacific, I slipped back outside the skin of the ship. Panama was indeed a forlorn place, one with all the sad hopelessness of the poverty around it, of people who lived in boxes, with trash and refuse scattered all over. There were dogs, kids, and people running aimlessly around while others tried to wash clothes or catch fish in the filthy water around them. Panama had caused a huge lump in my throat and a deep sadness, as well as a profound thankfulness. My belly was full every day, my clothes were clean, and I had a nice place to sleep.

What we didn't have on this ship was positive morale. But knowing we were closer to our new home was enough to keep us all going. One huge luxury that really helped was having a phone on the mess decks, and permission to call home.

My mom sounded so happy to hear from me. The few times I could afford to call she always asked where I was, and it was funny because every time you could hear my dad in the background shouting, "Sher, she can't tell you where she is!" No, I couldn't tell them our location because of security purposes, but it also helped that I had absolutely no clue where we were anyway. We could have been in the Sea of Tranquility on the moon doing circles around the earth and I would have had no idea.

# CHAPTER 18

# Pierside in San Diego
# and San Francisco

**B**esides having problems with a vindictive chief and a set of equally vindictive senior chiefs, not to mention the other grudging sailors I had worked for in my division, I also began having major problems with my hands. They suddenly quit working. I couldn't hold anything in my hands, and I began dropping everything I tried to hold. The pain from my thumbs and middle three fingers felt like sharp electric shocks running from the tips of my fingers, to my shoulder, and the pain and inability to use my hands became alarming.

In sickbay, Doc lightly tapped on my wrists, and the pain was immediate and electrifying. It was all I could do to beg him to stop. When he had me gently flex my wrists as far as I could, I couldn't flex far before both went numb.

I joked, "No way it's carpal tunnel syndrome. It's a brain tumor, right?"

"Looks like carpal tunnel syndrome." Apparently scrubbing floors and Deep Sink washing had torn the life out of the median nerves in both my hands; they were tired of being compressed like pancakes, and just gave up completely. I had to have my wrists bound in a 45-degree angle twice a day for the next two weeks, and then I was fitted for splints when we reached San Diego.

I took the light/limited duty chit Doc also gave me and handed it to the mess decks 1st class, who then unhappily passed the bad news onto the *Dark Overlord*. He threw a huge tantrum. He railed and complained all the way up the chain of command and back again, claiming that I was "worthless to him," and "that I should go back to my division." Everything seemed over to me here.

But sometimes it's the people who are quietly in the background pulling strings who matter the most. I had no clue that someone in charge of this whole department had noticed everything that had been going on. From what I've heard from other shipmates there were decent sailors with good intentions who executed plans to remove me altogether from the mess decks.

Looking back it was obvious how I quietly accepted the vindictive way that the *Dark Overlord* had treated me, and I had handled it with grace even going above and beyond duty when it called for it. At one point when a large ship-wide inspection was eminent some fellow shipmates were upset that they had so little time to repaint the entire passageway on the portside of the ship stretching from the mess decks all the way back to amidships. I softly volunteered my services and they watched with shock and wonder as I managed to cut and roll the entire space, turning everything including the overhead from a dingy dirt-cast to a bright and clean white in only a few short hours. I saved the day, so to speak, and got attention while not wanting to or needing any pats on the back. Luckily the right folks took all this in and intervened on my behalf.

Had I a decent and competent chain of command in engineering I might have wished for their plans to include returning me to my division, watch, and firefighting duties. After all, I was the one most qualified to stand watch in my division, and I had successfully trained a team of firefighters who had passed inspections. But the reality was I worked for the most retaliatory chain of command and they made it known they didn't want me back.

Instead, I was sent to the ship's laundry. A 1st class named Lynda taught me the ropes, so to speak, which included the washing and drying of massive mountains of laundry from everyone onboard ship every day: no small task. But she showed me how to pace myself, and I stepped into the task and applied myself setting aside the pain in my wrists. The threat of going back to my old division and being back under Chief Malvado's thumb kept me on my toes.

Laundry was an unexpectedly amazing place. The people I worked with were fun, and the eight-hour workday couldn't be beat with a crowbar. But the best part was the chain of command here was outstanding. So I really worked hard, sometimes even when my wrists hurt so bad I had to grit my teeth and kept going. Lynda pulled me aside one day. "I want you to know that I see the work you are doing back here. I will take care of you on your evals. You are one of the hardest workers I've ever had."

She let me soak that in, like she knew what a shock it was for me to get any honest feedback. After a small pause she added, "I don't understand why the folks in your engineering chain of command complained about you, and told me what a problem you would be. You've been anything but." I took that to heart; it made me quietly proud to hear someone offer such generous praise, and to see me, possibly for the first time since joining the Navy, as the sailor I truly was.

Now fifteen years after I'm not angry, *much*, at the many wrongs, imagined or real. What I'm most angry about are the friendships I missed out on. I wish I could go back and be who I am now. I wish I could slow myself down and enjoy the friendships of the many outstanding shipmates I served with, and get to know them better, instead of feeling as if I had to guard and protect myself from everyone. I wish I could go back and open up to Lynda about the massive secrets I had been holding onto.

In late May 2002, we transited into San Diego and I was awash with all sorts of emotions over being physically around Malvado again. I avoided him as much as possible, but when our paths crossed, his scowl was an indicator that he would catch me later. The ship didn't stay longer than a week or so in San Diego, which is affectionately called "San Dog" in the fleet, but I admit I was really looking forward to our second stop—San Francisco.

The morning we were scheduled to pull into port we all put on our whites to proudly *man the rails*. Manning the rails is an old Naval tradition evolved from the centuries old practice of *manning the yards* where men on sailing ships stood evenly spaced on all the yards and gave three cheers to honor a distinguished person.

So there we were, resplendent in our dress whites, standing in a line arm's length from each other, and occupying all the space around the gunwales or edge of the ship. I was standing back aft, on the flight deck, with a large group of other shipmates, and the excitement was tangible. For many of our young crew this was our first port outside the fleet.

As we went under the Golden Gate Bridge I remember looking up at it and feeling awe: we had worked so hard to get this ship seaworthy, and we had put up with so much crap from an awful upper chain of command to get to this point. And here we were, about to get away from them for another port call: the feeling was pure exhilaration.

After we passed underneath the shadow of the bridge I looked back and the rising sun reflecting off of it was so gorgeous. I will never forget that sight. The dark azure blue of the water, the bridge over it a bright copper red, glowing in the dawn light. The contrast was amazing, and made me catch my breath.

As we passed Alcatraz, I realized what a fitting metaphor it was for my life. I'd felt locked up inside myself for the past year, and I knew there was no escape from that prison. I knew if I gave up what I was hiding I was going to sink with it. And in a few short months, I would.

San Francisco, meanwhile, was a lovely place to visit. We pulled in to berth in the cruise ship area in Pier 35, just to the east of the tourist-friendly Pier 39 and Fisherman's Wharf district. I went out into Chinatown and walked the streets, joining up with my best friend, Dave, to bar-hop.

After a few bars, we decided to stop at a convenience store for Mandarin Absolute, which, when added to orange juice, made a killer screwdriver. We went down by the water's edge and sat on a bench and relaxed, watching a just-married couple standing along the water's edge. Dave laughed as he hooted "Good Luck!" at them. Sitting there, Dave recounted how he saw one of my 2nd classes holding another shipmate's hand as they walked through town in identical Alcatraz shirts. "And then that fucking Chief Malvado came face to face with me earlier today," he said.

I felt sucker punched.

"Apparently he's pissed off that we're hanging out. He fucking caught me alone in the Log Room checking my email. He challenged me, told me I need to leave you alone. I was like, 'Why, Chief? So you can bother her? I am keeping her out of fucking trouble. Thanks for your concern.' Then he tried to have a stare-down with me, before tucking his tail between his legs and leaving. That guy is beyond fucking unbelievable."

"What should I do?"

"I don't know because when this goes south, it'll go bad for you the most. The good ole boys club protects their own."

We sat awhile in silence, both of us likely imagining possible results from protection of that good ole boys club. We were so young; I was twenty-two and Dave thirty-two. And, yet, we both felt so old. I think the military has that way with most of us, of aging us beyond belief in a short amount of time. Nothing lasts. Not the length of life, or silence. Eventually everything must be broken, and as we realized this was the edge of brokenness, we sighed and headed back to the ship. There was nothing to do but to keep going.

A few days later, the ship pulled away from San Fran and steamed toward the horizon under the Golden Gate. As we drew closer to our new homeport in Washington everyone became giddy; we cleaned, painted, and polished—all of this to a definite neurosis.

# CHAPTER 19

# Homecoming and Commissioning

It was a cold day in the middle of May 2002 for our grand homecoming in Everett, Washington. We'd been told to report to the weather decks to help man the rails. So there we were, freezing in these transparent polyester summer dress whites, coming into Everett. It was raining pretty hard, and even though we were soaked and shivering, we were happy to finally be there. I remember wishing I had grabbed my warm, wool pea coat out of the sea-bag storage in berthing. A sizeable crowd standing along the dock greeted us as we pulled in, and I was disappointed for a moment that none were waiting for me.

As soon as possible, I headed back to berthing, dodging the crazy crowd, to change from my uniform to civvies and go join Dave at the bar on base. By this point, I was well aware my drinking was getting out of hand, but I didn't care. I just wanted the shreds of my soul to survive even if they had to do so through a gray haze.

Everett was pretty much still the same old Everett I remembered as a kid. I was surprised to recognize the old paper mill down Marine View Drive, and the old metal bridges over the Steamboat slough heading out of town. Even Paine field was still there. Everything seemed like it had been stuck in a time warp, except that a Navy base had been added to the middle of it.

Around the second week in June we were underway to Seattle for the commissioning ceremony of the ship. We parked ourselves in front of Safeco Field, the baseball stadium at Pier 37. We busted our backsides to get the ship ready, scrubbed her up, painted the inside all neat and white, and swept out the huge parking lot where everyone would be sitting.

The next day we all jumped out of racks and *turned-to*. It was insanity down in that teeny space. Every woman was crammed in our teeny head, trying to shower or put on makeup; it was chaos. Uniforms hung all over the berthing like huge white flags and if there weren't gals trying to shine shoes or iron in the cramped space then there were soaking wet towels bumping into everyone. Before long, everyone was generally frustrated.

Luckily, I had thought to shower the night before and all my neat uniforms were waiting to be put on along with polished shoes. I got dressed and neatened up my rack fast before exiting the scattered noisy mess for filter shop where I fixed my light make-up with a small mirror. I was good to go.

The uniform of the day was full dress whites, which included the high-necked "chokers" for the chiefs and above. I went outside the skin of the ship to do a quick one-over of the parking lot where all the chairs were set up and was not waiting too long when my parents showed up. I was so happy to see them. Dad and Mom were both wearing dress casual outfits, and looked sharp standing next to me. Chief Malvado noticed me hugging them and walked over, introducing himself. My bubbliness quickly shutdown with the shadow of this man falling across me, cutting between my parents and me.

Dad complimented me on how sharp I looked, and how exciting this was, how proud he was. Chief agreed with him, and then with one last glance at me he turned and walked away, thankfully taking his shadow with him. My mom would later comment on his odd behavior, how he acted like he was hanging too close to me, like a buzzard in a tree. She was quieter, more serious, watching me, and she noticed how the smile and mirth I had first shown melted the instant I saw Malvado. I felt as if she had turned me inside out with her eyes and had been able to guess the truth. Dad, however, had changed the subject, focusing on other things. It was a welcome distraction.

It was exciting and busy with what seemed like an almost endless flock of people crowding around the ship. We would learn later that about 5,000 had attended our commissioning event. When the announcement came for the ceremony to begin, we quickly took our seats. It began with the delivering of the principle speech from the commandant of the Marines. "This ship builds on a long legacy and will soon be the embodiment of the power of our naval teamwork." After another ten minutes he finished with an amazing send-off saying, "Throughout the world, she will sail with confidence in the defense of our freedoms, representing our 21st century answer to those who would threaten the promise of democracy and our freedom—still mankind's best hope for the future."

Then the two ship's sponsors came forward and were introduced. These were the wife of an admiral and the Marine granddaughter of the ship's namesake representing her grandfather. I remember how much I admired her. Here was a brilliant woman with a successful career in the military, standing proudly in her gorgeous dress uniform. I couldn't help but feel pain in my heart as I asked myself *What is wrong with me? What has she got that I don't?*

After listening to their words we then had to suffer through a set of completely unoriginal speeches from our ship's captain and XO, and I noticed I wasn't the only one fighting to stay awake. But we knew we were getting close. I tensed up knowing things were about to get super exciting.

At our cue we went running in our best-pressed full dress whites up the middle row of all the seated guests onto the ship to stand at attention, *manning the rails* in rows as we had practiced. Then the ship's bell dinged four times, announcing that the spirit of our namesake had just come aboard to inhabit the ship until the day she is decommissioned. After this the ship *came* to life; the gas turbine engines fired up, smoke billowed from exhaust stacks, and the radar started turning, all to signify the spirit of the namesake taking over the ship. Everyone in the audience seemed pretty amazed that we had gone to pains to coordinate everything.

After it was over, my folks took me out to a nice steak dinner. Afterward, I went back to my ship and got ready for getting back to the other side of Everett at the base the next day. I woke up to a brand new day, putting on my dress whites again, and getting to work. It was freezing cold that morning as we broke free and got underway. I remember feeling this air of déjà vu as we came into sight of our port in the chilly weather, finding myself wishing for my damn pea coat yet again.

My dad had told me the name of their hotel, and when I went over to starboard side of the ship, I could see the little hotel in Mukilteo where they were. Dad was on the porch, taking photos and waving. He seemed so proud, and I felt so dirty from the depth of secrets stirring around inside my gut.

Dad and Mom came to pick me up a bit later, and we went out for the day. First, we went to La Conner strolling about from store to store. Dad went on about how proud he was of me, how he couldn't believe his daughter had helped build and commission this amazing new destroyer. He told me again of how both Mom and he were so proud of me, and it swelled up my throat. I felt like a liar and a fake standing there with everyone proud of a person I knew I really wasn't. I was heavy with the ordeals of the past year that I endured.

# CHAPTER 20

## I am an Airplane About to Crash

Right after commissioning, the command decided to let us get underway for Victoria, British Columbia. I went above decks to check out the Canadian base at Esquimalt. It was a smaller base than Everett. There were two short piers and one really large building, and two beat-up, ancient, baby-blue colored frigates at the pier across from us. So, to say we stuck out like one big haze-gray thumb is an understatement.

Dave had to leave at the last minute for a family emergency, so I went out with six other shipmates from the boat—a tall, older sonar tech we called Fish who led our group; followed by two young shipmates named Jimmy and Jack; who, along with my friend, Spook, brought up the end with another shipmate from his division as well as a Boatswains mate. *What a motley crew,* I thought.

We took our time walking the 2.8 miles to Victoria. It was a great day for a stroll under bright and clear blue skies. The air was crisp, and the town clean and welcoming. As we got into the city limits someone noticed that it was almost noon. Someone else noticed a couple of nice places for lunch and a brew. So there we were, making the first stop of the day at an inviting pub and grub with an amazing view on the waterfront for lunch and ales. It was doubly convenient because Jimmy, the youngest shipmate within our group, insisted we stop and wait while he ran into Radioshack. Fish said, "We'll be over in the pub then. Don't get lost." And our group headed for the pub.

The pub was deliciously bright and enchanting with its warm and wonderful citrusy smell from the house ales brewed over the years in large stainless steel vats. Surrounded by this homey atmosphere we walked up to the bar and began relaxing and sampling various brews.

Fish, the most senior among us, dominated most of the conversation with his easy chatter about pubs and the lifestyle he had enjoyed during his time being stationed in the UK, and between the ale and listening to his voice I was relaxed and ready to fall asleep.

Jimmy's manic return not too long after pretty much ruined that. He came in with this ridiculously large electric airplane to which someone from our group shouted, "What are you going to do with that thing on the boat? Tow it behind?" Everybody laughed. He shrugged and sat down. He stashed the plane behind his chair so as not to disrupt the flow of foot traffic.

After we had a nice lunch and a couple nice, strong ales, we made our way closer to downtown Victoria, stopping occasionally at various pubs, meeting up with a lot more shipmates along the way. We split up when we got to the downtown area; half remaining together in a pub and the five youngest of us continuing on to sight-see while it was still early.

Our sightseeing group included Jimmy and his airplane, then Spook and a younger subordinate of his, and Jack. We headed first to Butchart Gardens and enjoyed a nice walk under pale sunlight. Clouds were forming, but we weren't in a hurry.

After a bus ride back to downtown, we walked through a large park and then Jimmy began flying his radio-controlled airplane; it actually had a pretty good arc on it. But at the last minute something went horribly wrong as the plane dipped, then stalled, falling out of the sky like a rock, coming down hard into the ground, dirt and parts violently thrown everywhere.

Everyone had a good laugh out of that, but Jimmy cussed hard about "a month's worth of pay gone down the shitter" and stood there with broken pieces and wings in his arms, looking as if he were about to burst into tears. I couldn't help but be struck by the depth of this moment; I was that airplane, flying somewhat wobbly, but stalling out and crashing hard. I could empathize with Jimmy, standing there with pieces in my arms, about to fall apart completely. I knew it wasn't going to be much longer. I was tired of hiding so much, telling so many lies to cover everything up, and feeling so much ugliness trapped inside of me. But after it all came out finally, people would laugh at me for a very long time; I would be a horrible joke to a lot of people.

As if an omen of those things to come from above, the sun disappeared, the clouds instantly turned black, and the wind came howling upon us, bringing with it a wicked cold front. We looked up at the sky just as thunder began crashing loudly and rain was spilling on us, soaking us to the bone and scattering us toward a warm, dry spot.

We quickly found a pub and trooped inside, and I realized my bra and shirt had become transparent from the rain. I tried to hold my arms over my chest when Spook began hitting on me. He was drunk, I told myself, and ignored him. But he wouldn't let it go, and his persistence was increasingly worrisome. He had a fiancée, after all, and I was in a relationship with Dave. Spook maybe knew this too. So again, I brushed off the inappropriate comments on our way toward a table. After dinner and more ale, we were warmed up and dry. The sun had re-emerged, and we continued our exploration of the city.

Along the way, we learned that the rest of our group was heading toward a bar called The Sticky Wicket, so we joined them. I remember hearing this name and saying, "Sticky Wicket? Sounds like something a guy caught in Thailand." And everyone laughed, because it did sound like a silly name to give a bar. Looking back I know now that a sticky wicket is a metaphor used to describe a difficult situation. And that was exactly the perfect set of words to describe the whole ordeal that was about to unravel even worse.

Evening darkness was upon us as we arrived at the large corner bar. As soon as we walked in it was obvious from the rock 'n roll blasting on the jukebox that American sailors had taken over the place. The large crowd sported military haircuts. In the middle of the crowd I saw Senior Chief Teasle, the man who had harassed me in San Diego over a year before.

Teasle was obviously drunk. He was hitting on all the younger women shipmates around him, and when he saw me, he waved. My friend Jack and I quickly decided to go to a dance club. As we walked out I turned to see that Teasle was coming after us.

I flagged a taxi, and suddenly Teasle appeared, yanking open the back door and falling inside, but not before grabbing my hand and pulling me in with him. He ordered Jack to grab the front passenger seat.

"Hey I jesh wan you to know you're a speshal gal." Teasle's arm went around me. "I been watchin you for some time and I haven't forgotten about you." His other hand slid up my thigh to my stomach and from there clumsily fumbled upward, trying to caress and fondle my breasts. I pushed his hands away. "Senior, please stop this!" But Teasle put his finger on my lips and stopped me from speaking. He was so drunk he wasn't taking no for an answer. When he attempted to restrain my hands in one of his, I yelled for the taxi driver to pull over.

My friend Jack was up in the front seat hearing everything, and trying hard to pretend he didn't. I was obviously doing something about it by stopping the taxi and getting out. I understand why Jack didn't say anything or try to stick up for me: it was this senior individual's word against his, and he didn't want to jeopardize his career. He was only the same age and rank as I was after all.

I climbed out of the car, and Teasle shoved his hotel room number he'd written on paper with the name of his hotel and his room key. "Come by later."

Meanwhile, Jack also exited the taxi. While we'd both had too much to drink, we weren't incapable of walking, or rather stumbling, back to our ship. Most of the walk back, my head was filled with nervous replays of Teasle's behavior. I'd been able to avoid him for months. Now the nightmare seemed to be starting over. When we finally reached the ship, I tossed the hotel information and room key in the water as we crossed a large bridge.

A few days later we were underway again for homeport after a brief stop at Indian Island that's located between Port Townsend Bay and Kilisut Harbor. Indian Island is a major US Navy munitions handling facility that receives and discharges munitions in support of US military operations worldwide, and all Navy ships stop there going to and from the ocean to load or offload munitions, depending on their orders and mission.

So our ship was moored to one side of the pier, and a small *fig* or frigate also from Everett was moored just behind us. What I didn't know then was that my future husband was also aboard that ship. He had left an aircraft carrier in San Diego for this small frigate in Everett about the same time I had left for Pascagoula.

Looking back everything makes sense now, even though for a painful couple of years I'd given up on the idea that God loved me. But in the years after the Navy, I've learned better. I've also learned that even though I couldn't see then the full unwinding of the mysterious way in which my life would intersect with others, or the *why*, God had a hand in all of it. How else to explain so many things that seem like mere coincidences? God has proved He exists. His loving hand was in everything. I would meet my husband later after we were both out of the Navy, and he would come into my life when I was truly ready to cross a threshold and begin healing from everything in my life including my childhood traumas. My husband would understand everything. And he would vindicate me.

It was the end of June when we returned to Everett. I made sure my work was finished, and after being dismissed, I promptly skated off for liberty.

I headed straight for the bar on base. Malvado and another senior sailor, Chief Yetzerra, were enjoying tall glasses of ale when I walked onto the scene. I picked a table all by my lonesome to sit, contemplate, and drink by myself for a change. It was karaoke night, so someone was busy slaughtering the hell out of a good Journey song. Malvado caught my eye and waved me over. You never publicly defy a chief, so I grabbed my glass and nervously walked across the bar. He pointed to a chair. The two chiefs babbled on about something, but I wasn't listening.

At one point, Malvado had to leave, so that left Chief Yetzerra and me alone at the table. I was about to get up and leave when Yetzerra laid his hand on my arm to reseat me. He said that Malvado really cared for me, and that he did too, and he was up for anything since the night was young. "Excuse me," I said, and left for the bathroom.

When I returned, I finished my drink … and blacked out. I woke some hours later sitting in Yetzerra's Jeep, heading *back* to base, wondering what the hell had happened. He said not to worry, he knew what all was going on between me and Malvado because Malvado had told him I was "a good gal," who could keep things on a "down-low." I barely remember him dropping me off in front of the barracks room I had rented for the night.

But the next morning as I walked to the ship in the chill of the morning, my mind was flooded with flashbacks: Yetzerra with his hands on me; images of him on top of me; lying on the carpeted floor in his empty house; so many tattoos across his heavy torso; his weight seeming to crush me; rug burns on my back. Had I been drugged? I must have been drugged. *What do I do now?*

When his path crossed mine that day, he smiled and went out of his way to get my attention and to be publicly nice. I spent the day in a fog of emotion and tears. What could I say? To whom? Who would believe me? "She asked for it," they'd say and stick up for one another. No one lodges complaints this serious against a twenty-year career chief without paying for it somehow, let alone two chiefs and three senior chiefs.

After work I returned to my room and finally worked up the courage to call my mom at the ER while she was working her twelve-hour shift. At the sound of her voice, I broke. I cracked so wide open that the sobbing made my story sound like incoherent babbling.

"Nicole, you've got to calm down, honey," she said. "Tell me what's going on!"

And so I restarted my story, the truth slowly dropping one word then one sentence at a time until the depth of my entire ordeal, from the first assault by Teasle in San Diego to the assaults by Malvado and the potential drugged rape by Yetzerra.

"Oh my God, Niki! You need to see a doctor!"

"No, I can't do that," I said. "I'm afraid for my life, Mom."

She replied, "Are you shitting me?"

In a teeny voice I heard myself say, "No, Mom, I'm not. This is a whole lot deeper than words. No one messes with these guys without paying for it."

"Nicole! You have to go to the cops!"

I didn't answer. I cried because there was no stopping it now that the truth was out there. I had never seen or believed in any viable options. Since the young woman's gang rape on my first base that went unresolved, I'd seen what happened to others who made complaints. Their careers, for the most part, were quickly ended. What hadn't dawned on me yet, and wouldn't for some time, was that I had finally told my mother and that *she'd actually believed me*. Later, I would see this as a turning point. On this day, however, I could only see a fork in the road leading to all places bad.

# CHAPTER 21

# The Very Last Straw

There was a 1ˢᵗ class on the mess decks who liked to flirt with me, but he understood boundaries. One day around the beginning of July he finally shed his pretense when he saw the right moment.

I was sitting alone at a booth in the mess decks when he came up and took the seat next to me.

"What the hell is wrong with you," he asked, "You have been sulking and quiet. You aren't yourself."

"I don't know what you're talking about."

He looked at me suspiciously, then coughed as he lowered his voice even more, confiding, "I have a very good idea what is going on—you and Chief Malvado."

I swallowed my heart and it got stuck in my throat. I didn't have to blow any whistles—apparently my shipmates were having a great time talking about me graphically behind my back to a select group.

After that he began to toe the water, working his way up to taking full-advantage of me, like the senior engineering guys were already doing.

When I was back on engineering watches in mid-July he must've waited for me, because he snuck down after me into the shaft alley, which was the one space on board ship that could only be accessed by one long single ladder climb down into it.

"Where do you think you're going?" he said in a menacing tone, blocking the ladder. "You're going to have to earn the right to go up this ladder."

I attempted to push past him. "You know," he said, "no one can hear you if you scream." And he was right. The machinery down there was loud. Also, he had made sure to dog the hatch before he climbed down after me. I thought about putting up a fight. I could have fought him. But I was afraid of the crazy in his eyes. In that moment I knew he could kill me and make it look like I had taken a hard fall off the long ladder to the bottom. And I realized I wanted to live no matter what I was subjected to. I was numb. It was better to shut down, dissociate, and let him do whatever he wanted. He ordered me onto my knees, and when I didn't, he pushed me hard onto the grating. As he began to unbuckle his belt and unzip his pants I lost all consciousness. Only fragments have ever returned.

Later he would boast that he was actually the main reason I got into laundry. I owed him, apparently, and payment was that I had to perform oral sex, or do whatever it was he said his wife would not do for him. And I never told Dave about any more of this. It was beyond insane and unbelievable—I sometimes felt I was making it all up. I didn't think Dave would believe what had happened since he was a good friend of that man.

But now in July, the theme was standing watches, hiding my miserable life, hoping no one could see the broken pieces crammed inside, and keep a low-profile. Every once in a while, Dave would get some time to himself so we would head back to his small space back by aft steering, where he had his gorgeous, purple, five-string Ibanez bass guitar chained up, along with his small Crate amp. We would sit while he played songs till his fingers bled. I loved it. To this day "Seek and Destroy" has a special meaning to me and Dave always played it along with every Megadeth song he knew.

What finally broke the wound open and raw happened exactly a month after we commissioned. It was by now the middle of July, and shortly before my birthday we were underway, about to come into Port Hueneme for a port call. A chaplain had also come aboard in Everett to enjoy the trip with us. All hands mustered on the mess decks where he introduced himself and told us we could talk to him. No matter what we told him, he insisted, it would remain a secret with him forever. I remember it was a Thursday when I made an appointment to speak to him, and then went back to my job.

I was called up later, and we sat down in the aptly named Burn Room, which was a space set aside for burning classified documents—his temporary office. I didn't know if I had the strength to open my mouth. Finally, I asked him several times if what I might share would go to the grave with him.

"Why yes. I will never tell anyone. What's going on?"

When I felt somewhat assured that it was safe, I spilled my guts. His eyes nearly popped out of his head. I confessed everything about the chiefs and senior chiefs and the other shipmates who had abused me.

The chaplain sat there, pale and speechless, and only came unglued after I finished. There he was, panicking, flipping out, saying how shocked he was and asking too many questions: "Who else knew, who else was involved? Are you serious? This is really happening?" After I assured him that I was not joking, that this had indeed happened, he assured me that I was the victim and he promised that he would stand by my side the whole time, and that nothing bad would ever happen to me.

But I knew what would really happen if I ever went public with my story. I hadn't even told him everything. Just most of it—to relieve some pressure from the burden I was carrying on my shoulders. Afterward, I went back to work.

Soon, the chaplain called me back up to rehash the whole conversation, and told me again how shocked and sickened he was that this had gone on for so long. When he asked if I wanted to come forward, I shouted, "No!"

"Don't you care about the other females on the boat, what if something was also happening to them?"

"With all due respect sir, but at this point I don't give a fuck about anyone else. I just needed to get this off my chest and to get on with my life."

He tried to push, cajole, and even guilt me into telling the command. And none of it worked. No way was I was going to let that happen.

Finally, he told me that there *was* one thing he could do.

"Listen, what I can do is to toe the water by letting the CO know about an *anonymous* situation going on, not give any names, just hint that there is a situation between a blueshirt and some khakis. Can we do that and just see how he reacts firsthand?"

"I'm not sure about this. No, I don't want to do that."

"Can we at least give it a try? No names. I promise."

I did not give him the go-ahead. But I guess he saw something in the way my head hung that said I was finished holding back hell itself, and he wanted to save me.

# CHAPTER 22

# How to Sink a Ship

The next day we pulled into port outside the Seabee base in Port Hueneme, California. The name Hueneme derives from the Spanish spelling of the Chumash word *wene me*, meaning *resting-place*, which I would later find ironic, given all that was about to happen.

Our ship was here to undergo operational evaluation of her missile systems—Naval history in the making. And here, my story was about to make history too. Seemed I had chosen a great time, or the worst time depending on your perspective, to confess to a Navy chaplain.

Here's how it all started—

I was cleaning my spaces on the ship, nearly finished with work, and looking forward to liberty. I heard someone shout my name. Then it seemed everyone was calling me up forward at the same time, as if my name had been attached to a significant fire somewhere.

I scurried to the mess decks, and found the 1st class who had assaulted me not too long before. He pulled me close and hissed, "What the fuck is going on? That chaplain is looking for you. Hell, everyone is looking for you! What is going on?" Something heavy dropped in my gut. I scrambled topside to find the chaplain. He was standing outside the Burn Room with a grave expression. "DCFN Strong, the CO has given me direct orders to have you stand outside his stateroom."

Tears began to well up, and I fought them back, burying my face, hot with fear and shame, in my hands. The chaplain put his hand on my shoulder. "You are the victim, and you have done no wrong. It is going to be okay now." And he escorted me to the CO's stateroom in officer country where he left me standing in front of the door in parade rest.

I have since spoken to chaplains who are colonels in other branches such as the Army and Air Force, and they have told me this Navy chaplain had no right to give up my anonymity. A chaplain has no obligation to take a direct order from a CO, but this Navy chaplain either didn't care or didn't know any better. I was physically shaking as officers walked by and did a double take. They knew something bad was about to go down.

How long I stood there I can't be certain, but eventually the CO walked down the passageway toward his stateroom and let us both in.

He ordered me to sit in a chair opposite him, and just then there was a knock on his stateroom door: the XO and command master chief walked in. I was surrounded by men with no way out but to give them what they wanted. Only this time it wouldn't be my body. It would be the truth.

So there in the CO's stateroom I told them about the rapes and harassment, all about the senior chiefs and chiefs. I sobbed, and apologized, and choked on the guilt, but I got the whole ugly story out in a palatable way. I don't remember much after that—not what they said or what happened next. What I do recall is being back in berthing, with my heavy rack open, hurriedly packing my seabag and telling the shipmate across from me that I was going on leave when she asked.

Senior Chief Walken ran into me, and I almost threw-up. I guess he had some idea of what had just happened because his eyes were huge and worried. But I couldn't look long at him. I was done hiding all these secrets. Everything was exploding from Pandora's Box now.

No sooner was the ship tied off than the chaplain had me whisked off under a cloud of personal numbness and gloom. It was a sunny Cali day, but for some reason or another I remember it all in grays and shades. It was also a July heat that I recall vividly as a cold blast of emotional winter. It was all frozen plain for me—I couldn't feel or see straight.

The chaplain had been assigned as my escort. He said he was taking me to a place where I was to stay until the command was able to get me a flight back to Everett on Monday. On the way we ran errands. I remember going to a little office area only vaguely, and then to the Navy Exchange for some quick items. Then he drove me on a seemingly endless road. I had no idea what was going on or where the hell I was going. And I didn't ask.

We came to a nearby Naval Air Station in Point Mugu and he escorted me to a room in the barracks where I was ordered to stay put for the next couple days. After briefly asking if there was anything else he could do, to which I could only shrug, he took off, leaving me with nothing more than a few dollars, a sea-bag with all my possessions, and a heart that longed to scream and be freed from the weight of guilt and hurt.

Inside I lay down on the bed, exhausted but unable to fully relax, in a state of continued shock. I couldn't believe this was happening. The adrenaline was flowing nonstop and I could feel the arrhythmic beat of my heart. I tried to sleep but my mind fought it. During the night I woke up in sweats, not remembering at first where I was.

I woke up the next day starving, and after sitting on the bed wondering what to do my cell phone suddenly rang. I burst into tears and hysteric sobs when I heard my mom's voice. I told her that everything was out on the table. "What is going to happen?"

"I don't know," I said, as it appeared my life was over, and that I didn't really know where to begin or end. But I was definitely more alone in my life, and hungrier, than I had ever been before.

"Why?"

When she learned that the chaplain had dropped me off in the middle of nowhere with no money and no way to be able to eat at the galley, she went into Air Force officer mode—meaning my mother who was also a physician, strong-willed, and intelligent with a degree of clinical bluntness, took control, and I was more than happy to turn over control to her at this point.

My mother called back later to say she'd called the chaplain and pulled rank on him. And it worked because he was on his way. Something hit me, and I felt incredibly secure for the first time in a long time. After we hung up, I sat on the bed, drew my legs up under my chin, and began to silently cry again.

When I was thirteen and upset after my uncle had tried to have sex with me, I finally told my parents. My mom sat shocked for a moment, and finally rushed out with my father in tow to another room. His face was ashen, but he never looked at me as he turned to follow her out of the room. So I didn't think they believed me. My uncle was right, I thought.

Nothing was said again, or done, and I was told to stop talking about it—let it go, everyone said. Family members looked at me as an attention-seeker, and one went so far as to accuse me of being a "willing victim."

I would learn years later after I was out of the Navy that my parents had believed me, and were crushed that their daughter had been molested. They felt as if they'd been attacked as well, and that they had failed to protect me or see the signs of the abuse. Years later my parents would finally hug me and tell me they believed me.

So to have my mom believe me about the situation on the ship at that time meant the world to me. It meant that I was going to get through this, that I was going to be okay.

After a short time there was a soft knock on the door. I looked out the peep, and made sure it was him. The chaplain entered with a sure swiftness, surrounded by an air of condescension and anger for having been bothered. He pushed a set of orders into my hand along with a box of breakfast bars. "You can repay me when we get to Everett, Monday", was all he had to say. Since my new orders included dining at the galley, I was able to head over for at least a salad.

After that I felt much better, and went strolling around outside in the burning sunlight. I walked around a small area where there were some tall pines growing. I saw an owl soundlessly flap away, and looked down to find a single, small owl feather, which I picked up. It reminded me of myself, and how I wished I could fly soundlessly away from here as well. I went back to my room and watched TV, until my cell phone rang.

It was Dave. "Still alive?"

"I guess."

"Where the hell are you?"

"Point Mugu, I think."

"Ah. Nice base, good surfing. I am coming over, you need anything?"

"Liquor. And more liquor. Surprise me!"

Sure enough, about twenty minutes later he came strolling in as his typical easy-going self, with the familiar blue bottle of good vodka and two shot glasses. We had so much fun that night getting drunk and playing our old drinking games. I loosened up. Then he told me how crazy the ship was—especially engineering. I told him I was afraid they'd make me walk the plank.

"Thank God, they stopped keel-hauling over a hundred years ago," he said.

We slept hard that night until there was a sharp knock on the door the next morning. I looked through the peephole and recognized our ship's legal officer. I whirled around and quickly whispered to Dave, "Oh shit! What do we do? He's here!"

"You tell him to wait and I'll make everything, including myself disappear."

I nodded and yelled through the door, "Wait one second, sir, I'm not decent."

"Fine. Just make it quick, please."

Dave quickly hid all the liquor and evidence of a party, and found that the door to the room next door was open, so he jumped in there and closed the door behind himself. The legal officer knocked much louder the second time, and called out, "Fireman Strong, open this door!"

I opened the door just as he was getting ready to knock again, and I didn't have to try hard to pretend I had rolled out of bed. I imagine he could see I had dark circles under my eyes and my hair was a wreck. He asked permission to enter so he could take down my story. "Aye, Sir."

I repeated everything I had told the CO, and the legal officer recorded it without making a comment. When he was satisfied that I'd shared everything, he gathered his things and left.

I opened the door to the next room and Dave emerged. "What the fuck! You're going to be famous if this shit keeps up!"

That jolted me. I didn't have to ask him what he meant as we were only a couple-hundred miles from Las Vegas, where the infamous Tailhook scandal took place some years before.

# CHAPTER 23

# My Sad Birthday

Monday—the middle of July 2002—was my birthday. I found myself turning twenty-three with numbness and aching bones. When most folks would be blowing out candles and eating cake, I was getting on a small plane out of the teeny airport in Oxnard, California, with the chaplain. It was surreal. I remember looking out the window as we flew over the sea, and there was my ship below getting underway. The dread I felt was insurmountable when it hit me that I should have been on that ship, not in the bind I was in.

So, later that day found me back in Everett, on my birthday, and there I was talking to a JAG officer (military lawyer) and it was the last thing I wanted. The JAG officer told me that this was a big deal but I basically had the right to not talk to Naval Criminal Investigative Service (NCIS) if they questioned me; however, I could still be punished if the command decided to overlook my statement of rape and chose to handle this in-house with a Captain's Mast; also called non-judicial punishment or NJP.

"NJP is not a trial," the JAG officer said. "The commanding officer does not require evidence of any wrongdoing. You won't get a chance to state what happened or defend yourself, and I cannot help you there. JAGs are not allowed to defend anyone at Captain's Mast. I highly recommend you not speak to NCIS though. There's nothing more I can tell you or do until we find out if it is going to court-martial. Anyways, good luck."

As I left his office I felt like luck was the farthest thing from my grasp. There was no one in the world to help me. I was on my own.

At the Naval base in Everett, I was placed in administrative hold and sent to 1st Lieutenant, or 1st Lt, which was the office that oversaw sailors who were injured, or in admin holds rendering them incapable of being on sea duty. There I joined the other sailors who picked up trash on the base, cleaned office spaces, and emptied trashcans. 1st Lt also loaned out folks who were able-bodied to do jobs for various folks on base who needed the help.

One day, I volunteered to help out in the barracks, so I went from picking up trash to scrubbing barracks walls, plastic plants, and filthy rubber floor trim.

Every morning for the next week I would look out my window, expecting to see the unique superstructure of an Arleigh Burke destroyer telling me my ship had returned. I hid everything under a thick mask of hard work and compliance. I knew something was going to happen, but not when, and the anticipation was eating me alive. I was allowed to wear my headphones, so I played Megadeth's albums *Youthanasia* and *Cryptic Writing* into the ground. Every time I hear them I am back there again, wondering what the hell will become of me.

Early one morning I woke up to find the distinct superstructure in the pier announcing that my ship finally returned to port. And, not long after I was ordered to go to NCIS. The ship's legal officer, as well as the ship's master-at-arms, were present during my appointment with NCIS. Both urged me to tell the truth after I was read my rights.

Read my rights? Tell the truth? Was I under arrest?

The detective explained that this was just protocol. But the biggest shock came when he produced a tape recorder. I said no, that I had already talked to a JAG, and he'd advised me not to say anything.

The detective said, "Okay, well we can do this the easy way, or the hard way."

"I don't want to do it any way, period."

"Okay. Fine." Everyone got up and left, leaving me sitting alone in the dark room.

This went on for a good couple hours, during which they denied me water, food, and bathroom access. They would return, apply more pressure by saying they knew everything anyway, and finally, the NCIS detective threw down the written version of my statement on the table in front of me. "You're wasting our time. You better start talking now. You can be court-martialed if you keep playing games. We can stick you in the brig or worse. We can play this until the bitter end. You will be the one worse for wear."

At some point that night I finally broke. I was such a wreck. I had told my story to the chaplain, and to the command, but now to be telling it to a NCIS detective under duress after having been basically threatened was beyond me. I was being treated like a criminal and I didn't understand it. Where was the chaplain who had promised nothing bad would happen to me?

The NCIS detective typed my statement, asking so many questions that by the time I was allowed to leave NCIS, I'd been there over fifteen hours.

A few days later NCIS loaded a lot of shipmates I knew from the ship, including my friends, along with the chiefs and senior chiefs, into a van, driven ultimately by Doc, the lead corpsman on the ship. Dave said he'd shouted "Shotgun!" and hopped into the front passenger seat. Nothing could bring that guy down, it seemed. He said later that he'd turned around to take it all in: Senior Chief Walken, Senior Chief Teasle, down to other shipmates in engineering who had ratted out other folks to get out of trouble.

Dave knew indeed what was about to happen. As he glanced around the interior of the van he knew who the real dogs were. He looked at Doc and said, "So we aren't going to medical, huh?"

Doc sighed and started the van.

At NCIS several detectives greeted my shipmates and separated them for interviews and statements. Dave said later that when he'd been asked what he knew, he said he hadn't any information, and that what he did have was hearsay. Apparently the NCIS detective slammed his fists on the table to get Dave's attention, but Dave wouldn't break. When it came down to it, the detectives tried the same tactics on the other men; this time by saying, "We will not only tell your wives, we will then court-martial all of you!"

Some of the guys caved, or tried to get someone else pulled in. But Dave didn't break; he told NCIS to go fuck themselves, and that he wasn't talking. When NCIS brought me back in, they told me they knew everything, and that if I didn't tell what the hell all was going on they were going to send us all to the brig for a long time.

He put pressure on me, trying to press my buttons. Eventually, I came unglued. I told him this wasn't about friends who I had told ugly secrets to. I asked him about the chiefs and senior chiefs, trying to redirect *him* for a change. This was what the whole ordeal was about, really: the rape and sexual harassment I'd put up with. He said he had talked to all of these men, and that they all had denied any wrongdoing.

But I maintained that the chiefs had sexually assaulted me, and that the senior chiefs had harassed me non-stop. The detective then changed tactics to appear more sympathetic. He asked me about everything in more detail, said that he believed me but he needed proof. I provided unusual identifying details about Malvado's genitals that I'd noticed in the dim light of the hotel room before he forced himself on me in Philadelphia. He wrote everything down, and finally dismissed me.

A few days later I was called back to NCIS to sign and initial the statement. But I noticed that a few things were incorrect, some incidents even omitted such as the groping incident by the senior chief called *Dark*

*Overlord* in the Pascagoula bar. When I asked why the groping incident had been omitted, the detective said, "Listen, the command is overseeing this, and they have the final say here. Honestly, you are in a lot of trouble and I don't care for your lack of respect. You sign and initialize this, or face court-martial. You've wasted enough time here."

"No, this is not what happened!"

"Relax," he said. "I am going to present this to the command that all these guys knew what was going on and took advantage of you because of their collective knowledge. Let's just sign this so we can get the investigation over with." So that was it. I couldn't see a way out other than to initial and sign what was more his version of what happened than mine.

A few days later, NCIS questioned everyone again—and again the chiefs denied the accusations, but added that I was fabricating stories out of a desire for attention. What I also wouldn't know until much later is that I couldn't have been court-martialed. Neither could Dave or my other friends. Only the chiefs. But we didn't know this back then.

Looking back at it all now, I wish I hadn't revealed that Dave had known my ugly secrets. I wish I hadn't admitted to anything other than to the bigger scandal that involved the senior chiefs and chiefs.

# CHAPTER 24

# Gagged and Bound, Castaway

Near the beginning of August, after NCIS was done with me, the XO came out to oversee things. Looking back, I guess he was worried that I might go to the newspapers. This was a bigger scandal than I had any clue of at the time. Plans were made to have me sent straight off the base the first chance they got.

I was told to pack and take orders to go to the Naval Air Station up on Whidbey Island. The ship's master-at-arms also explained that I was under a very serious gag order and warned me severely not to say anything to anyone or I would face terrible repercussions. As I drove across the base, with endless airplane hangars and dark trees, what should have been relief was insurmountable dread. I had a horrible feeling in my bones that this was going to end worse than the whole ordeal put together.

I was put to work at the aircraft firefighting school way on the other side of the base. The team of sailors there were really professional, and no one bothered me. I got to wear a thickly-lined silver proximity or *baked potato* suit and light the fuel that came sloshing out of siphons on the large airplane-shaped scrap of metal with a big butane torch, so the classes could learn how to work together to put out a very possible casualty onboard an aircraft carrier or gator freighter, even a destroyer like mine, on which the dangerous job of landing a helo happens.

One day the chiefs wanted me to light the scrap metal for a class, and they wanted me to approach it a certain way. The wind coming over the sound was powerful, and when I walked toward the siphon it began sparking toward me, which meant the raging inferno would be terrible for the unprotected men just downwind of me. I backed out fast and the chiefs began shouting at me at for defying orders. But after that encounter way back in San Diego with the valve, I trusted myself, and I knew all of them would have been fried. I turned and walked around to the up-wind side of the scrap metal and safely lit the raging fire. I was a Navy trained firefighter, after all, and I wouldn't do anything I didn't feel was unsafe or wrong anymore.

After the class fought their fire, the senior chief instructor called me to his office. I was expecting the usual ass-chewing. Instead I heard, "I want you to know I am very grateful for your having the common sense to disregard an order. You saved lives. You would have been fine, but the men right behind you would have been burned over with the direction the wind was blowing."

He'd nailed it: I would have been safe in my heavy suit, but what a horrible disaster for the other men down-wind of the hot flames.

"I am a DC-man, that's what I was trained for."

"I want you to start teaching classes first thing starting tomorrow," he said and handed me a set of red coveralls to wear. "You're one of us now," he added. "Dress like it."

I was a Damage Controlman, and I knew as much about firefighting if not more than they did, so they were pretty happy to have me around. This, finally, was the Navy I thought I'd signed up for.

A few weeks later the fellow instructors were going to the gun range and invited me along. Out of twenty-two men I was one of nine who earned a rifle expert medal. That was huge moment of pride for me, then and now. It was a nice diversion, pretending to be a normal person who had a wide-open future. I was doing a good job at the fire school, and now I had earned a coveted ribbon, and things were looking up.

In the middle of October I thought that the whole situation had a hope of a good ending. I lay in bed relaxing with a book after a long day when all of a sudden that ominous sound of my phone ringing shook me, and every last good dream I had was dashed when I answered the call. It was the ship's master-at-arms calling to break the bad news that I was going to Captain's Mast the next day. That night I gathered up my things, opened my window, and tossed everything out. From there, I dragged my belongings across the lawn to my truck in the parking lot, to go back into an empty room to lay awake all night crying, wondering how this was going to go.

# CHAPTER 25

# Captain's Mast: Shock and Awe

The morning of October 17, 2002, per instruction, I appeared at the shipyard in my best full dress blues.

The command had set aside a double-wide trailer in the shipyards to serve as their mess decks and this was now the location of the Captain's Mast. Nearly everyone from our ship had been ordered to attend this public display of humiliation. It began to rain, and I tried to focus on the view across the sound of Whidbey.

I stared blankly out over the dark green water at Whidbey Island. I wished I could go back there, go back to yesterday when everything had felt somewhat normal before the master-at-arm's call.

The door opened, and the master-at-arms called, "DCFN Strong! Front and Center!" as if I were a hundred yards away and not standing within a few feet of her. I had no idea, frankly, what to expect from this. I headed up the middle of the two large sections of chairs that were occupied by my fellow shipmates. I marched with my back straight, my chin up, and my head back. I focused on the sound of my medals, swearing I would maintain my military bearing to the very last moment if it killed me. Everyone swiveled in their seats to observe my entry. The rifle medal I earned while on Whidbey awaiting this kangaroo court clanged loudly against my other medal, and I was grateful. *See what I've accomplished in spite of everything?* I wanted to shout. *You cannot break me. I will survive.*

I reached the front and stopped before Captain Redlight, who was looking down on me from behind a tall podium. I realized my cover was still on as I rendered a salute, and it felt wrong; no one wears a cover or salutes indoors in the Navy, unless at a Captain's Mast, and I had just passed this landmark. Captain Redlight's tone and demeanor scream that he is about to make an example of me.

"DCFN Strong, you have been found guilty of twenty-five charges. These range from indecent acts with another, to fraternization, to adultery and sodomy. I cannot believe this was going on like this and no one knew it!" And as if I've instantly become clairvoyant, I can read the minds of every senior sailor in this room who had observed the CO's hypocritical behavior up to now: *The CO continually set a piss-poor leadership example with his own public adulterous relationships. What did he expect?*

The CO's dark face glowed bright red and he pounded his fist on the podium. He raised his hand and pointed to me, denouncing me as a disgusting example of filth. That I have slept around the ranks, going right down gunnery and straight up engineering like a cheap whore. He accused me of destroying his ship and ruining unit cohesiveness. After he finished publicly demeaning me, he added, "For these atrocities you committed you are being awarded a punishment of sixty days restriction, loss of one half month's pay times two, and you are further reduced in rate from E-3 to E-2 again. You are hereby dismissed! Get out of my sight!"

And with that, I turn and make the long walk back, bearing the weight of a new reputation: not as a rape victim, but as the whore who brought down a ship.

Next, they called Dave front and center. When he got before the CO, Dave didn't mince his words. When he was given permission to speak, Dave came unglued: "With all due respect, Sir, but why am I getting in trouble for what these damn senior chiefs and chiefs did? Why are we being held as examples when there are at least a dozen officers I know offhand who are screwing enlisted folks? Not to mention our senior officers are screwing around. This is a bullshit witch-hunt."

The CO sputtered and attempted to redirect, but Dave had already made his point. He was the only one among us with the balls and brass to defend the truth and stand up for me. The CO knew Dave was pointing a huge finger at him, and he knew he had to send a message to everyone that no one is going to complain or talk about anything. No one is more credible than the CO, after all. So, he busted Dave's crow from 1st class to 2nd class, and another friend from 2nd to 3rd class, all for standing up and knowing what was really going on, or having anything to do with my situation. It didn't matter who was who. If you were a friend of mine, you were going to burn on the same pyre I did.

Later, the stories would emerge about what was happening behind the scenes. That this was a huge sex ring, and I was the instigator. Others would say I deserved far worse than the sixty days and loss of pay and rank. Another bunch of shipmates would accuse me of getting all these guys drunk, and after having sex with them, then calling "foul" out of regret.

Looking back, I think a lot of shipmates were angry seeing that supposedly *good men* were getting into trouble, and most of all, seeing a situation that reinforced why women shouldn't be in the Navy, or why no one complains about sexual misconduct, *period*. I know now that a lot of senior shipmates knew what the commanding officer was doing was absolutely hypocritical, and it would probably be why my ship would be the only ship he would command, even as he ended up being promoted to just under the admiral ranks. But what happened to him was light compared to the punishment and treatment he gave me.

And it was the same with the other senior men. The *Dark Overlord* who groped me in the bar in Mississippi would receive a complete pardon. Senior Chief Teasle and Senior Chief Walken would receive letters of reprimand—their dispensation held over to a later time.

Since the ship in the yard was next to the Naval base for repairs, the entire command was living in trailers next to her. I'd been given my own room, and after the Captain's Mast, I was setting my gear on the bed in my room when the master-at-arms appeared with a needle and thread in her hand. "Take that third stripe off all of your uniforms," she said, pointing to my left arm. She rattled off a list of my new boundaries, which included keeping my door locked at all times, and she walked out, slamming my door closed.

I fought through the shock while removing all my rate badges to reveal my new E-2 rank. When it was time to remove my E-3 rank from my dress blues, I finally burst into tears.

# CHAPTER 26

# A New Day at Midnight

After noon muster, someone knocked loudly on the door to my room. Through the door I heard the gruff familiar voice of the ship's master-at-arms. I opened up and let her in. She preferred to stand inside the door frame to tell me to pack up again: "You are going to be taken across the sound to Bremerton to finish the remaining fifty-five days of your restriction there. We were able to get it worked out that they will take care of you. You will be on your best behavior. Any complaints will be handled drastically," she warned in a deep growl.

I nodded and packed up, secretly relieved and elated to get away from everyone here. Some of my fellow shipmates had been horribly cruel in the things they whispered and I overheard them when I left my room to go to meals or to use the head. Others had been cold, acting as if they didn't even see me, and making it clear they wanted me to see this. It was a dichotomy that I didn't exist to some, but did to others merely as fodder for torture.

Other than these incidents, restriction was no big deal. Everyone had to wear neat uniforms and gather with the ship's sheriff for muster several times a day on time to be inspected. We had no freedom to do anything, which didn't matter anymore to me. For the past year I had no freedom anyway while under the thumb of a possessive and jealous man in my chain of command. I was told I was pretty much on house arrest, and was not allowed to leave my room without permission, even to use the bathroom facilities. Apparently, the command was afraid that I was a flight-risk, that I would hurt someone, or that someone would hurt me. I didn't ask, and I really didn't care. The master-at-arms stressed again that if I screwed up in Bremerton, I would be going to the brig next time with bread and water.

By then it was the middle of October 2002. The master-at-arms escorted me to Bremerton and it was late at night when we reached the base. The next day I was sent to the Mail Room, which turned out to be a stroke of luck. Mail Room was full of cool civilians working there: a guy named Pete, who, along with four other guys, supplied the seemingly endless amounts of mail for all the installations and commands on base. Pete didn't want to know my story, but he didn't need to; you could see the rivers of blood and defeat in my eyes. So, he took it upon himself to use his humor and good-naturedness to uncloud that river, to re-infuse hope back into my soul. I was going to live.

He taught me how to organize the mail, but he really didn't care if I did anything or not; he knew, in some way, that I had been through a God's honest amount of hell, and putting too much pressure on me would just be worse. Pete became my Guardian Angel, and to this day I am thankful to him for the mercy and care he took with me. I got my bearings back and began to heal.

When I finally had the guts to call up that chaplain, he answered and I asked if he knew what happened.

"Yes, I heard you had been sent to mast." He sighed. This infuriated me.

"Sir, do you recall way back when I told you about all of this, that you told me you would be there for me. You said I was the victim, remember? You said you would never leave me?"

"Yes, I did."

"So what happened to you? With all due respect, but you abandoned me here, so you could pat yourself on the back and be a hero." He was speechless, but I made my point. When I hung up, I realized everything had gone sideways as my friend Dave once said it would.

Midway through my fifty-five days was Thanksgiving. One of my close friends, Justin, from Whidbey, took the ferry over to surprise me. I was so happy to see him that I hugged him so hard he joked about not being able to breathe. We ate turkey at the mess hall, and it was great to catch up with him. It gave me hope that life wasn't over, that I still had friends who cared, and I could move upward and onward. I had not called my mom to tell her the outcome of all this. I couldn't face her or my father, or the humiliation of telling them I had been found guilty of anything.

On the very last day of restriction as I checked myself out, I also got my things together in the mail room and said goodbye to the men who treated me well there. As I was about to leave Pete handed me an envelope with my name on it.

Inside was a heartfelt card with, "Good-Bye! Everyone here will miss you!" And on the inside, "From the big wheels on down ... to all the loose nuts!" I had no idea what my future held but I knew I would never forget the kindness that I had been shown.

# CHAPTER 27

# The Court-martial

In December 2002, I was finally off restriction and taking the ferry back to Whidbey and back to the same room with the same cool roommate. I was happier than I'd been for a long while. I had lived through hell, and survived. I thought things were looking up. But I had no idea that life was about to take another bad turn.

It was déjà vu all over again. I was in my room on Whidbey when my cell phone rang. It was the master-at-arms dropping the bomb that I was expected to testify in January at the courts martial of the two chiefs. And this time, I actually experienced my first nervous breakdown. The base psychiatrist at Everett placed me on medication, but I heard him in another room discussing my "issues" and saying that he thought I was "faking it." I never returned to his office.

When I finally called and told my mom everything, she was silent with the consternation of someone who has known something bad was going on but not knowing exactly what. When she discovered the drug I'd been prescribed, she demanded that I stop taking it, immediately, before I ended up with permanent twitches in my face. But she couldn't undo what all had happened.

Before the legal proceedings, the prosecuting JAG attorney had words with me. Apparently, he had good news and bad news.

"All news is bad pretty much, for me," I said.

He laughed and said the good news was that I wasn't able to be court-martialed; I told him I knew that already.

"So what's the bad news?" I asked.

"Well," he said and fidgeted uncomfortably, "You might have a virus you need to get seen for immediately. It appears the chief in your chain-of-command who assaulted you had HPV."

"Say that again, Sir?"

"You have been exposed to a strain of human papillomavirus. And it is a very aggressive version at that."

I would almost have preferred the court-martialing.

The court-martial was held a few days later in a small courtroom inside the large admin building. I had been falling apart, having nightmares. I didn't know if it was the weight of everything caving in finally, I just knew that there I was in my dress blues yet again, having to endure the thought of facing the man who had assaulted me and stalked me, and tried to play games with me for almost a year straight.

I reported to the legal office where I was told to have a seat in the office waiting room. I did so, taking a seat across from two other women sitting there. As I sat there, I realized with horror that the women were the wives of the two chiefs. And they knew who I was and why I was sitting there, and I listened to them whisper about me. They hated me, and looking back, I don't blame them. They had to hold together somehow as this was all dropped on them like an airplane in their backyard. So, to keep going they had to accept what their husbands told them and think I was the one in the middle of everything.

This was a bitter moment that reminded me of one like it back in 1998. The Clinton sex scandal had hit the mainstream media. I remember hearing the president himself lying under oath in court, and I remember his wife standing by him, even after he was proved to be lying on a large-scale. When the women began coming out of the woodwork with stories of long running affairs as well as harassment and rape, I vividly recall the reactions of that man and his wife to silence these individuals, to settle out of court, and to publicly disgrace anyone who might speak out against them. The impeachment trial alone left a large imprint on me: the president was found guilty of perjury and yet no action was taken. He was allowed to finish his time as president leaving office in January 2001, as I was in the Navy, and about to undergo my own scandals. And here I was, now being called to witness against one of these men, having to face him one last time to end everything.

The court martial opened that morning and I was called as a witness. As I seated myself I looked down and saw the man responsible for why we were both here. Chief Malvado looked down as his lawyer maintained his client was pleading not guilty. But he was guilty, and he was here, and I never thought I'd ever be in the same room with him again. Suddenly the reality of the hell that I'd endured the entire year hit me and I broke down in tears. The judge stopped everything to ask if I was okay to finish my testimony. I tried to calm down and move on to the line of questioning the prosecuting JAG was asking but I broke down the whole time, nodding and saying "yes" or "no" to his questions.

The prosecuting JAG had issues with stuttering and with his voice cracking, dropping papers, and excessive use of the word "um" before everything he said. This was his first time in court. The judge, a captain, shook his head after the young officer finished his nervous spiel.

In the end both chiefs were found guilty of an "unduly familiar relationship" as well as "fraternization" and ended up with a mere slap on the wrist. The second chief supposedly accepted a plea bargain, pleading guilty of lesser charges, skipping court-martial and accepting punishment of brig time to keep his career intact. He was later re-stationed in San Diego. Chief Malvado was busted to E-6 and forced to retire. While that sounds terrible, he still retired at chief's pay because of the "high year tenure" law, which was in effect back then, allowing anyone with three years or more in a pay grade a retirement salary at that pay grade no matter what.

That the men who raped and harassed me were allowed to walk free on minor charges was salt in the many wounds I was trying to heal.

# CHAPTER 28

# The Crow-Killer

In May of 2003, I'd been working as a Navy journalist for a while, because they were extremely shorthanded, and I felt jaded and worn out, although I was more stable than I had been in a long time. I thought the worst was over, and I could look forward to being re-stationed to finish out my remaining enlistment. So I was floored hearing that my command was trying to process me out of the service. What had I done to deserve being kicked-out, especially when almost all the other senior men were allowed to stay in? Looking back, it's obvious: the command used me as an example to send a message to the rest of my shipmates that no one would be tolerated talking about anything. And when the command had the chance to cover everything up by kicking me out they took it.

After work in the middle of May, I was walking across the parking lot to my car when I heard a familiar voice. I turned and saw my old best friend, Dave, standing there. I thought he hated me for having been humiliated and busted down in rank all because of me. So I didn't know what was going to happen here. We both stood silent for a long moment before Dave finally broke the ice.

"Nic? How-how-how you been?" he stuttered.

"I've been better. How have you been?"

"The same. I've been wondering about you. I've missed you."

I ran over and hugged him. "I missed you too. It's nice to see you again."

He walked me over to his Bug and invited me out on the town. I hopped in and we went out on the town playing our little games like it was the old days. We got a room to crash in down at the officer's barracks over in Smokey Point. At one point we watched music videos, drinking vodka, and he began to speak, trying hard to express something I could tell was hard for him.

"Hey Nic, I want you to know, I don't forgive you. And you have to understand how I mean this."

"What?" He put his hand up to signal there was still a more important moral of the story coming.

"I don't forgive you because there's nothing to forgive you about. Nothing was your fault. That's what I mean. Those chiefs and senior chiefs were fucked up pieces of shit, and the command was just as big a piece of shit to blame everyone else for it, especially while the Captain himself is out fucking around. We all made choices but some were way guiltier than others. Don't let anyone fucking tell you any of this is your fault. It isn't. Ever."

Hearing this was profound. While his words didn't fix anything, they did begin to change how I looked at the situation much later on.

At work I was assigned base duty driver as one of my last jobs and it was an easy job until shipmates from my ship got in. Hearing them whisper about me, calling me a bitch, or a whore, calling me a "crow-killer" was one of the harder moments I ever had to muster the strength to get through.

But I did it, because I'd focus on happier times instead. Happier times during childhood when my dad would pack us kids up and take us places with him. We'd spend summers on the family farm hours north of Green Bay, waking up in sleeping bags to the lazy putt-putt-putt sounds of old John Deere tractors in the background, and the warm hay smell of cows around us. I loved running free as a kid all over the place, and when my dad decided to teach me to shoot an old .22 rifle he'd found I was actually a good shot. After that he'd let me shoot pigeons that huddled on the old silo, or kill crows that came to make a mess of my uncle's garden. Killing crows and pigeons was something I was good at, and a foretelling of things to come.

Because here I was, wearing a rifle expert medal, and the word "crow killer" was now an insult, a term meant to represent something far more sinister as I realized the crows I had "killed" were the ones that had been on the arms of my closest friends when they were busted in rank at Captain's Mast because of me. And I really felt that it was my fault.

The pain was excruciating, realizing all my shipmates who had been my friends now hated me; that my name was forever blackened by people who either sneered at or laughed over it as if I were a cheap joke. I got through that day, but I was never going to make it if I had to go through it again. So when sailors were needed for bearing arms at military funerals I stood up and volunteered myself.

Before too long it was the beginning of June 2003, and I was told that I would be meeting with a representative from my ship the next day: the sailor in charge of all enlisted record keeping.

He was a chief, a quiet man with a shy smile, and everyone on the ship liked him, spoke highly of him, and I conceded him that. However, I could see that the nice guy was not here before me. It was the same person but with a tangible cloud of contempt and irritation. He would look in my direction but focus on some point behind me the whole time.

I carefully took the seat in front of him, his face flushed and his eyes flashed icy and cold as he stared off at the wall behind me. His forehead furled as if he was holding back some deep-seated emotions, maybe hatred, or revulsion. He continued to stare off into space as he shuffled his papers and hurriedly began to address me.

"Okay, DCFN Strong, I am here to tell you that the Command recommends you be separated from the service."

"Why? I want to stay in."

He rolled his eyes, cleared his throat, and took a look in my direction as if to say, *Well, look at yourself.* I was very worn down by this time. I was pale as a ghost, and having nightmares and rage issues I did not understand.

"Well, the command considers it a good recommendation, since if you did remain in service you would find it very hard to outrun what all happened on the ship."

"Honestly, I don't care about their recommendation."

"Okay, well then maybe this will help you. If you don't sign this paperwork and you interfere with just accepting the discharge you are being offered you will be sent before an admin board, and the discharge they will give you will be much worse. I think you need to think this over. Staying in is no longer an option."

His words were a blow in the center of my chest. My mind went crazy with emotions and questions that were racing by. "What kind of discharge will the command recommend for me?"

"That has not been decided yet. I am just here to have you sign the paperwork to initiate this process. You're the one who ultimately decides how simple this can be."

"So I have no choice here, I am not going to be allowed to remain in the Navy no matter what?"

"Not under any circumstance. But you do have a choice between having the board hear you out. I would not recommend that since the command will provide all records including NJP and charges and evidence against you to the board members when they review this."

He didn't even look at me as he blandly laid the paperwork down and set a pen on it, and pushed them across. He didn't even have the courtesy to hand it to me. I took the pen and after several hesitations, my shaking hand signed and initialed on all of the lines where there was a purple *sign here* sticker. I pushed it somewhat back, my eyes threatening tears.

He grabbed the papers, shuffled them around, stood, and pushed his seat under the table.

"Okay, DCFN Strong, we are through here today. I will be in contact with you when we get the rest of the paperwork back and have a definite day of discharge for you." He turned and walked off promptly, even then, unable to look at me.

It was the middle of June, exactly a year after we had commissioned the ship, when the chief returned with the paperwork. I read through it all, realizing with utter horror that I was being kicked out the very next day, and had been given an Other Than Honorable discharge, which was being levied on me for "Serious Misconduct."

"I can't believe the command is doing this to me."

His body language revealed a total lack of empathy.

The source of his disgust could be found in the comments of the commanding officer.

It read:

DCFA Strong demonstrated a callous disregard for the rules governing good order and discipline and respect for the differences in rank. Her escapades, which she knew to be against US Navy Regulations and USS Zevel guidelines, resulted in letters of reprimand for two E-8's, Special Courts-Martial for two E-7's (one of which was reduced to E-6), and the reduction in rate of three E-6's to E-5 and one E-5 to E-4.

Her desires and need for attention, in addition to ruining several careers, has created a chasm throughout this Command that has yet to heal.

She failed to show remorse for her actions and waived all rights regarding her administrative separation processing per enclosure (2). She acknowledged that by waiving all rights her characterization of service would be Other Than Honorable.

In accordance with reference (B) and enclosure (2), I strongly recommend that DCFA Strong be separated from naval service and receive an Other Than Honorable characterization of service.

I was dumbfounded. I felt like screaming and throwing things and burning the place down.

The next day I vaguely remember being told I needed to turn in all my uniform items. I was outside my body, watching, wondering how this was possibly happening.

I reported to a 2nd class who explained that she had been given the task of checking me out and making sure I left base with no issues. Furthermore, I was to get up to my barracks room double-time, clean it up for inspection, change into civilian clothes, and have my complete sea-bag full of all uniforms ready to turn in for inspection.

She dismissed me and I did as I was told. I cleaned my room spotlessly, and after changing clothes began to pack my sea-bag, cramming it full of every uniform I had ever had, including the expensive working whites I had recently purchased.

Inside I said "Fuck it" and kept my gorgeous pea coat, belt buckles with a destroyer and *plankowner* underneath them, and some of my coveralls and dungarees, not to mention my first ship's ball cap, along with almost all my sea-bags; and, along with the medals I had earned, I also kept the silver Navy eagle pin from my dress cover.

The 2nd class quickly inspected my room and stomped off, taking me back across the base for the last part just before seeing me off at the front gates.

Finally, she told me to get my car.

"I'll meet you over there, outside the front gate. I have to do something first."

So I drove out and sat there waiting for her, and finally she appeared with a razor.

"What am I supposed to do with this?"

She pointed at the windshield of my car.

"See that DOD decal? You need to scrape it off, and I have to watch. Now go do it. Hurry up. I have other things to do."

I took the razor and scraped off the sticker.

The 2nd class turned and left without a word. I took a deep breath, got in the car, and drove off in a cloud of thick lingering fog, feeling weird to be free, lost, and trapped all at the same time.

# EPILOGUE

# Rising from Ashes

It's 2018 now, over fifteen years since I left the Navy. I find myself standing in my large, warm bedroom, in the middle of winter, in the middle of the night, but inside me is a long running warmth and love that no amount of darkness or coldness could destroy. I lay down in a handmade pine bed next to a wonderful man, my husband of over five years, who has given me the best seven years of my life.

Because looking back it was precarious for a time.

After I found myself lost on the other side of the wall in June 2003 I fell into the lowest gutter. I was able to get back into the Union but I was not able to carry on like a normal human being. The stress of dealing with people, with situations, and having non-stop conflict broke me down horribly and I eventually found myself out of work and out of options. I turned to stripping and prostitution to survive because there were no other decent jobs for someone kicked out with such a repugnant military discharge as I had been given. It was an ungodly time for me. I was a lost soul, alive, but on fire with hate and lust to find meaning for my existence. I did a lot of ugly things that I am not proud of, and I misused my body out of survival.

I went from being a proud Navy sailor, to a construction worker, to a stripper and a hooker, in short to no time, performing gut wrenching and vomit inducing acts in exchange for sustenance; humility doesn't breed such a lie. But numbness and desperation do.

I find this part of my life has only created a deep running compassion for everyone around me, and when I took off the black hateful mascara once and for all, I began to love again, and not just myself or my family members but everyone around me. I had been to the depths of hell and I understood what it meant to be in a dark place on the edge.

It was then I finally hit the ground, on my knees, and said the first prayer I had prayed in what seemed like decades:

"Lord, please. I know I don't deserve anything from you. But please help me to love and live again!"

And help came to me; out of the blue a door opened as my phone rang. It was my dad calling. He told me he wanted me to come home. I listened and cried.

So in October 2003 I was on my way across the country, running from myself, and from all the ugliness and injustice I had just been cut open from. I didn't deserve my family's mercy.

I felt I had, in so many awful ways, let them down and I didn't want to ask anyone for anything. I thought it was part of my punishment to have to gut it out on my own. But I was losing my light inside and beginning to fade. I needed help. And I am thankful that God and my family never gave up on me no matter how ugly or difficult I was.

Back in 2004 what saved my life was that the Veteran's Administration saw everything in my service record, including the awful words written by the Commanding Officer of my ship, who tried to serve me a crushing blow but only made everyone in the outside world realize how he had placed the blame for everything, and everyone's careers upon my back. They saw it for how it really was; that I was junior personnel, who reported sexual assaults, and the command did nothing to substantiate my allegations. The command punished me and kicked me out.

Thanks to the VA, I was quickly awarded a monthly disability amount for Post-Traumatic Stress Disorder (PTSD) due to "severe military sexual trauma" (MST) as well as damage to my wrists and other issues. I wake with the same amount of guilt and thankfulness every day knowing I am taken care of but there is nothing that can make a person forget the amount of injustice and inequity that I experienced. I spent the next eight years lost and angry, on various awful combinations of antidepressants and benzodiazepines by the VA. I was the closest thing to the walking dead you can imagine.

But on the good side I would also go through two discharge upgrades before I finally won the right to call myself honorably discharged, which everyone around me thought was the greatest victory. Oh it was, but I would still stumble horribly for a good many years. I would lose one nice house, go through two divorces, and then three hospitalizations for complete mental breakdowns and a failed suicide, but the worst was losing custody of my son over it all. I struggled horribly with suicide and self-hate and hatred of everyone, myself in particular.

In October 2009 my old roommate, Kelly, somehow found me and came forward to tell me some horrendous incidents that had happened to her shortly after I left the ship in 2003. At one port she was staying by herself at a hotel, and a 1st class broke into her room and ended up raping her. She never told anyone.

Instead she kept quiet for the next seven years until we met and spoke again. What hit me in the chest was when she told me, "I saw what they did to you. We all did. After that was over no one wanted to ever speak about anything. And things got worse." Hearing her tell me this broke my heart. It also enraged me and was the kick I needed to motivate me to really begin healing, so I could tell my whole story once and for all.

In 2010, I moved across the country to attend a VA in Sheridan, Wyoming, which had the best mental health facility for PTSD and Military Sexual Trauma (MST). Besides meeting my present wonderful husband, I got in a long line for the women's Cognitive Processing Therapy (CPT), which was one of the hardest things I've ever gotten myself through. It was two long months staying on the dormitory grounds at the VA, and going to therapy, classes, and groups starting every day at 6 a.m.

On St Patrick's Day 2011, I graduated and walked off that campus and found I didn't fit my old life. I realized what a lie I'd been living, that I had allowed myself to believe that I was weak and had no control over anything. I had also accepted the lie that I could never heal.

Around this same time I began having nightmares and flashbacks of the sexual abuse from my childhood. I decided to confront the uncle who had really cut me in half so long before. He denied everything. He was married now, with kids, and tried to tell me that he had PTSD from Desert Storm and didn't remember doing any of this, and he didn't believe he would do such a thing.

I was adamant about getting my point across, and after his wife and my grandmother rallied on his side, he came back twice as strong. Now it became an angry shitstorm, and at one point he threatened that if I ever spoke of anything, or tried to sue, that he would counter-sue and take me for everything. He told me I was a screwed-up kid who lied for attention.

Unbeknownst to him, my sister came forward, and spoke to my dad and confirmed my story, because she had been there and witnessed a lot of it. She backed me up, and it actually was the best feeling of vindication. From that day forth, the sun began to shine on me more as I took control of my life. I actively began to seek healing and love. And I began to miraculously heal.

So here I am, in the middle of nowhere, waking up next to a tall, handsome man, who works hard, doesn't complain, and has a pretty easy-going, conflict free attitude about life. We're both Navy vets, and we get each other's sea stories. I love listening to his; he has just shy of ten straight years at sea so he has an endless supply of anecdotes. It's obvious God has plans and lets people get so close to each other without knowing it—heck we probably walked by each other a dozen times and never knew it. I still have so many friends, most of them old shipmates and other folks I've met who are all veterans. We all share that common bond associated with military service, of knowing what it means to lay our lives down for a moment in time to protect the ideals of the whole.

One thing that survived unscathed through the years was the close friendship Dave and I had. We spoke several times a week for years, calling each other to check in, talk about the latest Megadeth album, or the military because he stayed in until his retirement in 2011. We were extremely close until he just stopped taking my calls in the fall of 2013.

After six months of not hearing from him I knew something was wrong. I went looking and eventually found someone who shared the news that my best friend, Dave, had died from a misdiagnosed brain tumor at the age of forty-three.

My heart is still broken and probably always will be. Dave was a larger-than-life man, and the world is less bright without him. Sometimes I see something that makes me want to call him up, and then I remember he's gone. And then my heart is broken all over again. Sometimes I am sitting in my car and a certain song comes on, and then it hits me that he's really gone and I start sobbing. I don't do this often. But grief isn't over just because years go by, or because someone thinks it's *healthy* to stop crying and to move on. Sometimes I am angry at the senselessness of his death. But it makes me realize my end might be around the corner. I hug the ones I love tighter and care more for everyone around me.

And life goes on.

We can't stop finding things to live for. I am now thirty-eight, and raising three beautiful children. I do art once in a while, and write, but mostly my life is spent in pursuit of our adventurous children, keeping a clean home and dinner cooked and on the table by the time my husband gets home. It's a good life. I never thought I'd ever be here, but it's nice at times when my mental and emotional states are cooperating.

It's at this crux where I have been made to realize the intrinsically important things, that life is not about making a living; that it is about living well, which has nothing to do with money or fame and everything to do with accepting a hard path gracefully and making something good come of it.

As far as my past, I am fully honorably discharged. I am taken care of. I won't say I am fixed, ever. But I am healing. The shadows and dark clouds still hang over me, and I still have bad days and I still break down under the heavy weight of a million pounds of anxieties that don't ever go away. It is work every day to manage everything, or to distract myself from the constant prodding of my past. It haunts me, some days worse than others. But I don't feel so destroyed over it anymore and most folks would never know I had so much ugliness if they met me.

I still have debilitating nervous breakdowns and panic attacks, especially when stress gets to be too much for me. Sometimes I have to torturously distract myself from the ugly memories that won't go away, the nightmares I still have. But this is a normal way to be after so much abnormal, and we just have to quit kicking ourselves and learn how to move on a little at a time.

It has occurred to me that if I hadn't gone into the Navy I wouldn't have any of the friends or good memories that I do enjoy today. It's taken a lot of healing and time and maturing to be able to admit that I don't regret enlisting anymore. Nor do I blame the Navy for what happened. The world is a terribly flawed place and you have to take the storms as they come and change for the better. Sadly, I wasn't the only person who was sexually assaulted, or mistreated. And my wish is that my story helps to validate the experience of anyone who is still holding too tightly to their own dark secrets for fear no one will believe them, and for those who want to give up. Maybe my story can give some guidance and hope to someone who has been through massive trauma and doesn't know yet how to deal with it all.

Anyway, I think the moral of the story is that sometimes one horrible thing happens in life, irrevocably changing us forever. We go through life not thinking about it—in fact we can cover it with dust but nothing is ever forgotten. At some point it has shaped our psyche in ways we need to face to grow. When more ugliness brings the old wounds back to the surface, we are given choices: face it, fight for meaning, fight for peace of mind and heal, or drown in the blood from the past.

I have had people tell me how brave they think I am, or what a hero they consider me to be, and I shake my head. I am no hero. I am not brave, especially in my own eyes. I am simply a person who endured a lot, probably far more than I should have, and I didn't give up for whatever reason. I saw no combat, or real war. But I've realized that my suffering is no less real, because sometimes the worst battles we fight are the ones inside of us.

I've been many things in life and been terribly unsure about my choices and myself. But now I have risen from my ashes because I have a purpose and I know who I am, finally: I'm a fighter who was once a sailor in the US Navy, and no one will ever take that away from me.

# ACKNOWLEDGEMENTS

My first round of heartfelt thanks goes to my editors—the amazing Tracy Crow and the outstanding Steven K. Allen. This book really wouldn't exist without either of them. Both of them cut through all the countless stories to show me the large stepping-stones on which to focus. I owe both of them so much for the healing and peace this whole process gave me: Tracy—for giving me my voice, encouraging me to forgive, and telling me not to give up; Steven—for having witnessed firsthand what I went through onboard our ship, reassuring me that all this really happened, encouraging me to tell this story, and providing guidance along the way.

My deepest gratitude then goes to all my shipmates and veteran-friends who have offered warm support of me through the years: Marcus Stevens, Crystal Thompson, Rob Wilder, Tarin Nugen, Edward Uptagraft, Harry Wilson, Christina Lievsay, Kori Burns, Donald Darcy, Grace Messerschmidt, Terri Myre, Tim Plank, Sonny Ayala, Colleen Ryan, Steven O'Briant, David O'Dette, Dustin Shepherd, Patrick May, David Butler, Frank Russell, Mike and Kristina Miller, Joe Aimone, Mickie Jackson, Jun Espanta, Chuck Bjork, Paul Cunningham, Carl Meyer, Edward Hackett, Derrill Floyd, Jessica Siewert, Terry McCalla, LeAnna Jarman, Kelly Hope Jackson, Jerri Bell, Marvin Cosby, Sam Millemaci, Eli Medellin, and Daniel Sanford, as well as all the other shipmates who made cameos in this memoir.

To several shipmates, I owe the deepest thanks:

One is my good friend Robert "Diesel" Cummins—not just for backing me up but for renewing my ability to reach out and trust again. Thank you, Diesel. You've helped me heal more than you know and I am so thankful to you for being here. I wish I could have worked for you in the Navy.

And a huge thanks to Charles Holmes and Clifford "Peaches" Haney for being amazing instructors who took an unsure new sailor and turned her into a tough damage controlman. Thank you for being outstanding examples of leadership.

I also owe my awesome friend, Nate Hale, the deepest thanks for being my friend and taking a wayward sailor and teaching her how to stand a proper watch and be a good snipe, as well as seeing the potential of that young woman and nurturing it. Thank you for being an exceptional example of leadership and for remaining my friend through the years.

I am also grateful to my other military veteran friends: Robin Parks Briggs, Tammy Elrod, Jeremy Stillwagner, Jenna Eatherton, Reid Reasor, Brooke King, Kathleen Hoffman, Fawn Mac, George Broadhead, Jeff Blankenship, Tanya LaVancha, and Richard Rossow.

I can't forget all the support from my wonderful civilian friends: Katie Devries Thrall, Glen Hazelwood, Lisa Parks, Terry Easley, Angi Rader, Jeannia Bressler, Mandy Bolte, Gini Mack, Terri Zerr, Phil Cummings, Kat Chisholm, Priscilla Humay, Paul Strong, Lisa Reinkemeyer, Debbie Gillespie, Shawn Mueller, Father Tom Miller, Gidget Macke, and Colbi Matheson.

I have to give a shout-out and huge thanks to Mindy Kuhn and her entire team at Warren Publishing for giving me this chance to finally share my story.

I am eternally grateful to my family—to my mom and my dad, my sisters and brother. Thank you for being there and helping me get through the past fifteen broken years while I healed.

I have nothing but the deepest gratitude and respect for my patient husband, Dustin, not just for giving me an amazing last name but because he really has been the greatest gift God could give any woman. Thank you for giving me the best six years of my life, for our children, and for the stability you provide all of us. I owe you the world, and I will spend the rest of my life thanking you.

And last but not least—to Aaron and Neil, my two shipmates and mentors who, sadly, are no longer with us. Every day I feel the loss of you. I hope to see you both again one day. Your friendships meant the world to me, and without you my story would be so different.

# ABOUT THE AUTHOR

Nicole Strong was born in Washington State, and grew up in Chicago, Northern Wisconsin, and St. Louis. She describes herself as a proud US Navy veteran, former wild land firefighter, artist, writer, and poet. Nicole lives near St. Louis with her husband and two children.

# WRITING PRIZE

For more than 250 years, American women have proudly and significantly contributed to the military in a number of ways, including combat, since the Revolutionary War. Their stories and contributions, however, have received little more than a footnote of recognition from historians.

Therefore, Warren Publishing, a woman-founded, owned, and led custom publishing company since 1988, has created the **Deborah Sampson Prize for Military Writing** and will seek to publish two contest winners per year.

## WHAT DO WE WIN?

Each winner will receive a $1,000 advance against royalties earned through a digital-first publishing format with a world-wide online distribution; Warren's award-winning editorial and graphic design support and marketing support package. *(A discounted print option is also available through Warren's hybrid author/publisher partnership.)*

## WHO MAY COMPETE?

American women military veterans of all ages and eras and women military family members (defined as parents or grandparents, spouses or partners, children or grandchildren of a military member who has served, or is serving in, the US Armed Forces) are invited to submit their book-length fiction or nonfiction manuscripts. Fiction may include a linked short-story collection or a novel. Nonfiction may include memoir or a collection of essays.

## SUBMISSION DETAILS

What to include on the manuscript's title page:
1. Name, mail, and email addresses
2. Telephone number
3. Title of manuscript
4. Genre (fiction or nonfiction)
5. Word count (minimum/maximum word count 40,000 to 80,000 words)
6. Double space and paginate the manuscript (please include chapters and paragraph breaks)

Submit only original, unpublished prose written by the applicant.

Please notify Warren Publishing immediately if the manuscript is accepted elsewhere during the contest period of deliberation.

Each entrant will receive general feedback (100-150 words) from its judge as to the merit and weakness of each entry.

Please visit Warrenpublishing.net for additional information and details.

Warren Publishing has a right not to publish, if no winner
is determined due to a lack of quality submissions.

CPSIA information can be obtained
at www.ICGtesting.com
Printed in the USA
LVHW11*2022011018
592071LV00001B/17/P